T0194235

A SHORT
SUPPORT FOR
SAME-SEX MARRIAGE

A SHORT SUPPORT FOR SAME-SEX MARRIAGE

RETHINKING THE TRASH TALK

STEVEN E. EIKE

This book is a work of non-fiction. Unless otherwise noted, the author and the publisher make no explicit guarantees as to the accuracy of the information contained in this book and in some cases, names of people and places have been altered to protect their privacy.

Archway Publishing books may be ordered through booksellers or by contacting:

Archway Publishing
1663 Liberty Drive
Bloomington, IN 47403
www.archwaypublishing.com
844-669-3957

Because of the dynamic nature of the Internet, any web addresses or links contained in this book may have changed since publication and may no longer be valid. The views expressed in this work are solely those of the author and do not necessarily reflect the views of the publisher, and the publisher hereby disclaims any responsibility for them.

Any people depicted in stock imagery provided by Getty Images are models, and such images are being used for illustrative purposes only. Certain stock imagery © Getty Images.

ISBN: 978-1-6657-5236-7 (sc)
ISBN: 978-1-6657-5237-4 (e)

Library of Congress Control Number: 2023920792

Print information available on the last page.

Archway Publishing rev. date: 11/17/2023

CONTENTS

ACKNOWLEDGMENTS

Not long ago, a young lady I love discussed her view that Genesis permitted same-sex marriage. I objected, using the usual pat answers. After the conversation, I felt uneasy about the practiced words by which I dismissed her thoughts. They were below the honor this person deserves, I thought. I began to investigate the topic. Maybe three years later, the result of my study has brought about this little book agreeing with her.

Same-sex physical love has become a volatile topic. I expected many would jump in with their deep thoughts. I was surprised that very few helped me with the topic along the way. Consequently, I am especially grateful for the feedback of one non-affirming pastor who urged me to read two evangelicals, Robert Gagnon and Stanley Grenz, whom he believes capture conservative thoughts against same-sex marriage. Refuting their thoughts against LGBTQ sexual practice became the focus of my research. I affirm my high hopes for their spiritual contributions in other areas. This book refutes each and every of their accusations against same-sex marriage as I have understood them. Thank you, pastor friend.

I thank my lovely wife especially much! Alice, you love peace and harmony! My conversations have, at times, been hard for you. God bless you for your endurance and affirmation! Thank you!

INTRODUCTION

God can bless same-sex unions. The Old Testament makes room for same-sex partnerships; the New Testament sanctifies them. Using historical-grammatical methods, this work produces undeniable reasons for reversing the tradition that condemns same-sex marriage. It exposes prejudices of past and present Scripture interpreters and some worldviews that misrepresent the text's meaning. The worldviews of ancient philosophers have derailed us from a biblical view of same-sex relations. We have been misled to condemn the innocent. The goal here is to expose the wrong-headed views of individuals and cultures of the past regarding LGBTQ sexuality.

The research herein closely reexamines the proof texts used by those, past and present, who condemn same-sex marriage. We will show their errors. We will show that God can fully bless a same-sex marriage.

This writing is academic. Our target audiences are those who want an analytical review of the best of literature for and against same-sex marriage and especially for those for and against who have an advanced familiarity with biblical studies.

THE OLD TESTAMENT PERMITS SAME-SEX EROTIC ACTIVITY

T he problem starts with a definition. The definition of homosexual that Western society generally accepts would not have been understood by ancient society or by Old Testament writers. No Old Testament word matches the definition of homosexuality that prevails in Western culture. That contemporary definition is roughly what Christian scholar Stanley Grenz calls a "predominant, persistent, and exclusive psychosexual attraction toward members of the same sex."[1]

Western culture widely calls same-sex marriage wrong, but the Old Testament does not present same-sex attraction as evil. In fact, no Old Testament passages even address monogamous, same-sex marriage. Interpretation of the Old Testament that condemns same-sex marriage stands on slipping sands.

---

[1] Stanley J. Grenz, *Welcoming but not Affirming: an Evangelical Approach to Homosexuality,* (Louisville, Ky: Westminster John Knox press. 1998), 32.

GENESIS ALLOWS FOR
SAME-SEX EROTICISM

C ontemporary church tradition forbids marriages of the same sex. Robert Gagnon, for example, speaks for church tradition, "Same-sex intercourse constitutes an inexcusable rebellion against the intentional design of the created order."[2] Agreeing with Gagnon, Richard Hays has written, "Scripture repeatedly affirms that God has made man and woman for one another and that our sexual desires rightly find fulfillment within heterosexual marriage."[3] In agreement with Gagnon and Hays, Stanley Grenz postulates a creation precedent: "God's intention for humankind as delineated in the Genesis creation narrative."[4] Is there a creation precedent requiring exclusively heterosexual

---

[2] Robert A. J. Gagnon, *The Bible and Homosexual Practice: Texts and Hermeneutics*, (Nashville: Abingdon Press, 2001), Kindle loc. 689 of 10277.

[3] Richard B. Hays, *The Moral Vision of the New Testament: a Contemporary Introduction to New Testament Ethics*, (NY, NY: HarperCollins Publishers, 2013), Kindle edition, 390.

[4] Grenz, *Welcoming but Not Affirming*, 54.

marriage, and how do God-given logic and scientific observation fit into the picture? When the relevant Bible passages are examined with position given to logic and science over tradition, the objections to same-sex marriage fall.

The Precedent Of The First Marriage
Allows Same-Sex Couples

A careful look at Genesis shows that it does not lay either an implied or a specific foundation to condemn monogamous, same-sex marriage. The Genesis introduction to marriage intends to be partial and situational. Genesis is an introduction; God's brief introduction both of himself and of his earthly work. As in any introduction, fine detail would bog down the story at the beginning. Instead, an introduction sets up the reader to understand the coming details. For example, the creation story in Genesis 1 does not include all of God's created creatures. Amphibians receive no mention. They do not fit perfectly as either land or sea creatures; they are both. Frogs will have their place in the story of God later on, but despite their absence from the creation story, there is no reason to consider the frog to be a creature existing outside of God's will. Neither are the details of Jesus' redeeming role made fully clear. Similarly, people may have a path that is not fully defined in Genesis. Roles may exist in God's creative plan that do not fit perfectly into widely accepted categories of male or female. In fact, no genetic template exists for a perfect female or a perfect male. Furthermore, it is unlikely that the genetic combination that was Adam and Eve has ever existed again. As time passed, Jesus affirmed eunuchs: those neither completely male nor completely female. Further along, we will explain.

So Genesis covers reality in broad strokes. Given the broad stroke descriptions of Genesis 1-3 and Jesus' affirmation of a separate group then known as eunuchs, we conclude that the creation account presents only the sex combination necessary to continue the story's plot development. Space remains to affirm gender diversity beyond the binary. Genesis leaves space for non-binary genders; people who are neither predominately female nor male may marry with the approval of God.

Western scientific research recognizes genders are not binary.[5] Science is one of heaven's gifts to humankind. The ability to see God's created order and draw reasoned conclusions is sanctified in Scripture, The heavens declare the glory of God (Psalm 19:1). In other words, the heavens and, by extension, all of nature declare certain facts about the universe. Intersex individuals confound scientific classification as either male or female. Megan DeFranza notes some reasons, reflecting on research, "The Consortium on the Management of Disorders of Sex Development lists the following as intersex-related conditions: congenital development of ambiguous genitalia, 'congenital disjunction of internal and external sex anatomy, incomplete development of sex anatomy, sex chromosome anomalies and disorders of gonadal development.'"[6] Certain types of conditions have been chronicled. Among the currently recognizable intersex conditions are Swyer syndrome (negligible gonad tissue development), Androgen Insensitivity syndrome (partial or

---

[5] Scientific method does not conflict with biblical interpretative methods. The supposed law of first mention is often applied incorrectly to the first couple. The law urges that within the first mention of any doctrine lay all the essential elements of the doctrine. First, the maleness and femaleness of Adam and Eve do not constitute a doctrine. They describe an historical reality. Second, the early chapters of Genesis are introduction and do not mean to originate detailed doctrine.

[6] Megan K. DeFranza, Sex Difference in Christian Theology. (Grand Rapids, Michigan: Wm. B. Eerdmans Publishing Co., 2015), Kindle edition, 24.

full rejection of male hormone action), ovary-testis combination (once called hermaphroditism), and atypical chromosome combinations.[7] The frequency of intersex occurrence may be as little as 1 in 1,500 as Down syndrome or as great as 1 in 100 like schizophrenia.[8] The evidence of these multiple variations acts to demystify same-sex attraction and reinforce its legitimacy. It follows that a mixed gender composition affects sexual preference. Variety in gender makeup means sexual desires will not necessarily follow outward appearance. Furthermore, since same-sex desire evidences itself early in human development, the human object of desires is not chosen but instead is inherent.

The interplay of mind and body during human development may also affect sexual preference. At this point, little has been done in the way of brain studies to clarify how the mind and body develop and work together to form sexual orientation. Research in this field called brain sex is in its beginning stages. "Brain sex may very well connect the dots between intersex and sexual orientation and gender identity, but at present, it is the least developed field of sexology and resists deterministic readings."[9] Those who inveigh against monogamous same-sex

---

[7] By limiting my descriptions, I hope to maintain the thematic flow of the thesis. Additional information can be found in DeFranza's second chapter, "Intersex: Medical and Sociological Challenges to the Two-Sex Model." DeFranza, *Sex Difference*, pages 23-67.

[8] Rates for schizophrenia and Down syndrome were drawn from Heather Looy, "Male and Female God Created Them: The Challenge of Intersexuality," Journal of Psychology and Christianity 21 (2002): 12. Looy cites M. W. Thompson and J. S. Thompson, Genetics in Medicine, 5th ed. (Toronto: W. B. Saunders Co., 1991). DeFranza, *Sex Difference*, 67.

[9] DeFranza, *Sex Difference in Christian Theology*, 267.

Steven E. Eike

marriage need to gain insight through scientific studies. As the study progresses, judgment should be subject to a scholarly reserve.

It is impossible not to assume from the early chapters of Genesis that heterosexual marriage will be a necessary and dominant expectation. Obviously, heterosexual marriage is part of God's plan. Gagnon is right to conclude that exclusively heterosexual relationships are portrayed throughout the Yahwistic source.[10] He is wrong to over-generalize from that, however. As the original couple, Adam and Eve had no chance to fulfill the physical part of God's plan to increase in number; [and] fill the earth (Gen. 1:28) without heterosexual conjoining. Nevertheless, a contingent who later developed with no desire for heterosexual intimacy would not have thwarted God's early plan to fill the earth. Therefore, when same-sex marriages are considered on the basis of the inability to procreate, they do not self-exclude from God's plan. In fact, same-sex couples can fulfill God's plan of fruitfulness (Gen. 1:28) by setting up a stable, loving home for fostering and adopting.

It is interesting to note and relevant to the discussion that the Genesis author promotes the essential similarity between Adam and Eve as most vital for completing human needs. Adam's joy in seeing Eve was because of their similarity. Until then, Adam had no one like him for companionship and help. Adam was very alone. Earlier, Adam was led to peruse candidates that were unfit to remedy his aloneness. Genesis 2:18-20 describe his ludicrous series of blind dates. Partnership with dissimilar creatures would not work. He would need a being akin to him (Gen. 1:28). It would be impossible for a human to make a satisfactory marital

---

[10] Gagnon, *The Bible and Homosexual Practice*, Kindle edition, ch. 1.IV.

relationship with an ape, for example. To give a silly application, in future days, how would they decide who gets the television remote? Lack of similarity makes humans and animals unfit for the helpful cooperation God intended. Adam's grand expression of satisfaction came because Eve embodied genuine companionability. His expression *at last* (Gen. 1:23, ESV) signifies that Adam recognized that his reviewing and naming of the animals had led him to the appreciation of the similarity of God's human helper for him. Wenham translates 1:23 along the same line, "This time! This is bone of my bones and flesh of my flesh!"[11] Adam's first thought may have taken him back to his review of the animals. But now he finally saw someone like him. John Walton is direct, "Adam's response to Eve recognizes her similarity to him."[12] Adam's joy came from his recognition of his similarity to Eve. If Eve were, in some manner, the weaker vessel, neither God nor Adam mentioned it. As to Eve's gender difference, while Adam would have recognized a reproductive difference within the pairs of animals, yet he comments on no such thing about Eve. Instead, the reader is shown Adam valuing the similarity between the woman and himself. The Genesis creation story highlights the similarity between Eve and Adam and makes no comment about differences, either anatomical or otherwise. As God tells it, the criterion for this couple's compatibility was their basic human similarity, not their anatomical difference. Adam's perceived need was basic; a helper way beyond an animal friend. God provided him with such a partner.

---

[11] Gordon J. Wenham, *Genesis 1-15 Vol. 1*, Word Biblical Commentary, (Grand Rapids, MI: Zondervan 2017), 105.

[12] John H. Walton, *Genesis*, The NIV Application Commentary, (Grand Rapids, MI: Zondervan, 2014). Kindle edition, 178.

Gagnon suggests that only a binary sexual pair can God's image. He claims "God's intent for human sexuality is embedded in the material creation of gendered beings .... 'Male and female he created them' intimates that the fullness of God's image comes together in the union of male and female in marriage" (not, he wants us to infer, from same-sex unions).[13] But Gagnon fails to recognize the implications of his proposal. If only a male and female in marriage can have God's image completely, then no unmarried person, even Jesus, could be fully in the image of God.

In the Genesis account of creation, there is no command to avoid same-sex marriage. In the early chapters of Genesis, God introduces himself to humankind in brief accounts of complex acts. He introduces humans to their intended role of blessing and nurturing his creation. Human reproduction will require males and females, but gender dualism is not the sacred pattern. To propose otherwise is to argue from silence and speculation.

---

[13] Gagnon, *The Bible and Homosexual Practice*. Kindle edition, ch. 1-II.

The Fall Allows For Same-Sex Couples

Before the Fall, God had declared all humans to be in his image. The NIV translation Genesis 1:26-27 uses *mankind* to mean all humankind. It is not only a male who receives God's image, but humankind, all people.

> Then God said, "Let us make mankind in our image, in our likeness, so that they may rule over the fish in the sea and the birds in the sky, over the livestock and all the wild animals, and over all the creatures that move along the ground. So God created mankind in his own image. In the image of God, he created them; male and female, he created them." Gen 1:26-27, NIV.

The first two chapters of Genesis introduce God and his relationship to his creation. Humans freely exercise their self-will. Only one prohibition is put upon them. They are not to eat the forbidden fruit. The Fall has everything to do with the trying of two humans and nothing whatsoever to do with future gender concerns as their population increases. The Fall narrative makes no suggestion that God imaged only binary genders or that he subtracted bits of his image from some humans. Nothing in the text supplies a touchpoint for that idea. Interpretative priority must be given to God's declarative statements, or we merely guess. The fall troubled all future life, but the fall did not curse same-sex love.

Eden had problems before the Fall. Having an evil being lurking in the garden as a snake signifies dangerous imperfection,

Steven E. Eike

and so do a pair of people who chose to disobey a good Creator. However strange it may seem; imperfection was part of God's plan. Therefore when God proclaimed the creation good in 1:31, it was because it well suited his divine purpose, not because it was objectively perfect. The conditions of Eden described in Genesis 2 do not illustrate a desirable state. It is important to note that God's ultimate resolution of Earth's problems promises more than just a return to imperfection in Eden.

The Fall did not incriminate same-sex attracted people. The genetics of people can mutate for good or for ill. Imperfection is part of God's plan. The original creation offered flaws for humankind to deal with. Those flaws likely included gene mutations that would produce a variety of changes; sexual variations among them. Does God not appreciate variety? People do not all look the same. Genes alter their appearance. The original combination of one man with one woman does not necessarily please God into perpetuity.

The Sin Of Sodom Was Not Same-Sex Desire

Same-sex attracted people are often associated with sodomites. That is a mistake. If we take the testimony of the Bible, something other than lusty attraction motivated the men of Sodom to seek same-sex relations with the visitors to Sodom. Hear the prophets.

Isaiah highlights Sodom's violence and lack of compassion, comparing Sodom's sins to Israel's of his time. He makes no mention of same-sex intercourse.

Hear the word of the Lord, you rulers of Sodom;

> Listen to the instruction of our God, you people of Gomorrah! Your hands are full of blood! Wash and make yourselves clean. Take your evil deeds out of my sight; stop doing wrong. Learn to do right; seek justice. Defend the oppressed. Take up the cause of the fatherless; plead the case of the widow. 1:10, 15-17 NIV

Jeremiah cried out, "The punishment of my people is greater than that of Sodom!" In context, Jeremiah sets the blame as evil deeds even among the priests, not because of same-sex copulation. Lamentations 1:6 Again, he says, "It happened because of the sins of her prophets and the iniquities of her priests, who shed within her the blood of the righteous." Lam 4:13

Ezekiel explained Sodom's sin to his generation, "Behold, this was the guilt of your sister Sodom: she and her daughters had pride, excess of food, and prosperous ease, but did not aid the poor and needy." Ez 16:49 The proud Sodomites blessed

Steven E. Eike

themselves but neglected the underprivileged. Notably missing from the "prophets' description of the sin of Sodom is same-sex desire.

Awkwardly, both Grenz and Gagnon make statements about Sodom that weaken their case against same-sex unions. Gagnon says, "While the story of Sodom, because of the added factors of inhospitality and rape, is not an ideal passage for studying the Bible's views on same-sex intercourse, it nevertheless remains a relevant text."[14] We ask why it is relevant? Gagnon further weakens his argument by shifting it to focus away from homosexuality to shaming, commenting they perhaps planned to use the heinous practice of gang rape to assert their superiority over and declare the subordinate status of the strangers... In short, showing utter disregard for the social rules of hospitality, they demand that the visitors submit to the most demeaning treatment conceivable.[15]

What does he think motivated the Sodomites?

Earlier, Grenz describes Sodom's treatment of others, "It would be to treat the conquered foe as a woman."[16] We will see going forward how little treating a foe as a woman relates to homosexuality. For now, we conclude that both Gagnon and Grenz are aware that same-sex desire does not capture the motivation for the Sodomites' attack.

The comments of these researchers hedge their bets. Neither Gagnon nor Grenz directly identifies the sin of Sodom as based on same-sex preference. For Gagnon, "The truth is that no one can say precisely how the Yahwist construed the motives of the

---

[14] Gagnon, *The Bible and Homosexual Practice,* Kindle edition, ch. 1-IV.
[15] Grenz, *Welcoming but Not Affirming,* 39.
[16] Ibid.

men of Sodom (beyond generic evil)."[17] Neither does Grenz equivocate when he concludes from all the biblical texts condemning Sodom, "We come away from these texts with a crucial question not satisfactorily answered: What about homosexual relationships between consenting adults?"[18] In other words, he asks for clarity about the very practice he opposes. Neither Gagnon nor Grenz shows the sin of Sodom is based on same-sex desire.

In Jesus' times, Sodom again was a byword for all that is evil and merits God's destruction and again the city is referenced without specific condemnation for same-sex eroticism. Matthew 10:15, 11:23, 11:24; Luke 10:12, 17:29; Romans 9:29 Jesus called out Capernaum's pride, not its sexual orientation saying, "Will you be exalted to heaven?" Matt 11:23 But Jesus, having seen the pride of Chorazin, Bethsaida, and Capernaum, foretold their end to be worse than that of Sodom. Matt 11:20-24

From the New Testament's perspective, the offense of Sodom was pride, lifting up self as the authoritative judge. According to Jude 1:7, Sodomites assaulted the bodies of angels. They indulged in gross immorality and went after strange flesh in the context of disrespect for higher beings. NASB Notice the repeated theme of arrogant rebellion in 2 Peter 2 comparing the Sodomites to those who were denying the sovereign Lord (vs. 1), depraved conduct of the lawless (vs. 7), lawless deeds (vs. 8), and those who follow the corrupt desire of the flesh and despise authority. Bold and arrogant, they are not afraid to heap abuse on celestial beings (vs. 10).

Jude and 2 Peter agree that Sodom proudly pressed for the extreme experience of dominating other flesh, even angels. The

---

[17] Gagnon, *The Bible and Homosexual Practice*, Kindle edition, ch. 1-IV.

[18] Grenz, *Welcoming but Not Affirming,* p. 40.

Steven E. Eike

Sodom event typified heinous wrong in the minds of ancient Israel, but the wrong was pride, not same-sex attraction. The New Testament does not point to same sex-attraction as precipitating Sodom's destruction.

Ham's Treatment Of Noah Was
Not About Same-Sex Lust

The failure of Ham to honor his father has no impact on same-sex issues. Gagnon believes Ham's story in Genesis 9:20-27 demonstrates a homosexual act so deviant that Noah cursed even Canaan, his grandson, the son of the perpetrator Ham. But was it so?[19] Ham saw the nakedness of his father and told his brothers outside [Noah's tent], Gen 9:22 He saw, and he told. Was homosexual desire the root of Ham's evil deed?

There are scholars who find same-sex rape in Noah's difficult moment and see a homosexual offense as the motivator of Noah's curse. Gordon Wenham sees the possibility of incest.[20] William Loader agrees that incest was potentially involved, "One might speculate that Ham not only saw his father Noah naked but also raped him." Gen 9:20–27[21]. But Loader sees the charge of incest as speculation. Scholars quibble about what seeing his father's nakedness means. Gagnon proposes that *seeing* is a euphemism for sexually acting out.

Gagnon believes Ham's act could not have been so small as mocking his naked father considering the strong penalty spoken by Noah against Canaan. Noah cursed Canaan to be a servant, in

---

[19] Gagnon, *The Bible and Homosexual Practice*, Kindle edition, ch. 1–III.

[20] Wenham, Gordon J. *Rethinking Genesis 1-11: Gateway to the Bible: the Didsbury Lectures 2013*. (Eugene, OR: Cascade Books, 2015), Kindle edition, ch. 3–footnote 47.

[21] Sprinkle et al., "Response to Megan K. DeFranza," in *Two Views on Homosexuality, the Bible, and the Church*, 110. Kindle Edition, 23.

Steven E. Eike

this case meaning the "lowest of slaves" to his brothers.[22] Gagnon quotes Donald Wold to explain, "Scholars who accept the literal view maintain that Ham only saw his nude father, but they must defend a custom about which we know nothing."[23] Presumably, this custom is that of using same-sex acts to undermine the power and reputation of another by feminizing their reputation. Following his tact, Gagnon proposes that a Mesopotamian omen text and the Egyptian myth of Horus and Seth are attempts at emasculating, disgracing, and demonstrating one's power over a rival. These texts illustrate manipulation, like Ham's act, to weaken another's authority, but they do not help specifically identify the act. We are supposed to conjecture that only by raping his father could sufficient shame be brought upon Noah to dislodge the senior's authority.

It is reasonable to suppose that Ham hoped to usurp the authority of his father and elder brothers, establishing his right to succeed his father as patriarch.[24] But Gagnon's claim that it illustrates the evil of all same-sex eroticism is a non-sequitur. It does not follow from the evidence he presents. There are many ways to discredit. Not only does Gagnon not prove that Noah was raped, but rape that seeks to diminish someone's power and authority has nothing necessarily to do with same-sex desire.

Gagnon also proposes a translation error to bolster his case that homosexual contact evoked Noah's curse of Canaan.

> Most important, the language of *uncovering* and
> *seeing the nakedness of* connects up with similar

---

[22] Wenham, *Genesis 1-15*, Kindle edition, 335.

[23] Gagnon, *The Bible and Homosexual Practice*, Kindle edition, ch. 1–III.

[24] Ibid.

phrases denoting sexual intercourse. Leviticus uses the phrase *uncover the nakedness of* to denote incest (18:6-18; 20:11, 17-21; also in 18:19, of sexual intercourse with a woman during her menstrual cycle). The same phrase is used elsewhere in the Bible of prostitution and adultery and of rape and/or public exposure for adultery.[25]

Nevertheless Gagnon admits that incest, not sexual desire may be the core of Ham's misdeed. As if to attack his own argument, Gagnon notes, "In Lev 20:17, the expression *sees his/her nakedness* is used to describe sibling incest; in other instances, the phrase *seeing the nakedness of* may imply an opportunity for rape."[26] Once again, if we assume for discussion's sake that Ham raped his sleeping father, nevertheless, the violations of Ham were incest and shaming, not necessarily gay eroticism.

Incestuous behavior was condemned in the Old Testament. It was subject to the ultimate penalty (Leviticus 20), whether same-sex or not. Consequently, even if Gagnon's evidence is correct, it still does not show that same-sex eroticism is wrong.

Can the severe curse on Canaan have been because of Ham's homosexual desires? We have not yet arrived at our evaluation of the two verses from Leviticus commonly used to condemn LGBTQ behavior. When we do, we will find that the verses do not refer to homosexuality at all. The English translations are in error. They do not mesh with the Hebrew text. As to the curse

---

[25] Gagnon, *The Bible and Homosexual Practice*, Kindle edition, p.77.
[26] Ibid.

Steven E. Eike

on Ham's son, a reader is aware that Noah knew his grandson from their time together aboard the ark. It is credible to think that Noah could see utterly unwholesome development in his grandson under the tutelage of Ham and project Canaan's future with assurance. The extent to which God honored that curse may illustrate the mystery of divine sovereignty.

Empathy and care for the dignity of parents were enjoined even beyond the boundaries of Yahweh's people. Wenham cites a writing from the 14th century BCE, "the Ugaritic Aqht epic.... states that a son takes his father 'by the hand when he's drunk, carries (sic) him when he's sated with wine'" (A 1.32– 33, ANET, 150). In other words, he must try tactfully to cover up his father's folly. But this is precisely what Ham did not do.[27] In his neglect, Ham's disrespect for his father is revealed. John Walton presents a preferred view as follows.

> Numerous interpreters have sought to read extra meaning into the verbs that describe Ham's activities in 9: 22, 'saw' and 'told.' The results have been incredible, insofar as Ham has been accused of incest with his mother, homosexual activity with his father, or even the castration of his father. Besides the obvious problems associated with getting these meanings out of these verbs, these sexual offenses are refuted by the fact that Shem and Japheth resist the offense of Ham by walking backward as they cover their father, which the

---

[27] Wenham, *Genesis 1-15*, Kindle edition, 335.

text says was done specifically so they would not see (with its conventional meaning).[28]

Ham mocked his father's compromised situation, but the profound disrespect of Ham for his father has no impact on same-sex issues.

---

[28] Walton, *Genesis*, Kindle edition, 346

Steven E. Eike

A look back at Genesis in light of the New Testament recalls the following.

- There is room in Genesis 1 and 2 for gender identification beyond dualistic male and female.
- Science finds non-dualistic gender makeups.
- The early chapters of Genesis introduce God's person and work in brief. Because Genesis is introduction, it describes events in broad, general terms. Many details are omitted.
- Returning to Eden is not a good option.
- Jesus widens gender categories to more than the two most acknowledged.
- Scripture labels Sodom's sin as pride, not same-sex attraction.
- Ham's offense against his father does not affect same-sex issues.

THE LAW DOES NOT CONDEMN SAME-SEX EROTICISM

Leviticus 18:22

Leviticus contains two significant passages that, in English translations, seem to address same-sex eroticism with a prohibition of some sort in both 18:22 and 20:13. The question arises, what do these verses condemn? Do these verses condemn homosexual eroticism, or do they make room for monogamous, same-sex love?

The context of the Hebrew Masoretic Text of Leviticus 18:22 applies to incestuous activity. A close view of the Hebrew text shows an important error in the translation of 18:22 in our major English versions.[29] The NIV renders it, "Do not have sexual

---

[29] Many commentators condemn all same-sex marriage without considering the translation issue, for example these three highly regarded scholars: Gagnon in *The Bible and Homosexual Practice*, Grenz in *Welcoming but not Affirming*, and Richard B. Hayes in *The Moral Vision of the New Testament*.

relations with a man as one does with a woman; that is detestable." The word homosexual misses the mark. K. Renato Lings' literal translation from Hebrew reads, "With (a) male you shall not lie (the) lyings (of a) woman. (An) abomination (is) that."[30] The words in parenthesis were supplied in an attempt to capture the sense in English. Eliminating the supplied words shown in parentheses leaves the command, "You shall not lie woman lyings." Robin Scroggs' translation agrees, "With a male, you shall not lie the lyings of a woman" (au. trans.) Lev. 18:22, or "A man who lies with a male the lyings of a woman" (au. trans.) Lev. 20:13."[31]

What are these woman's lyings? Lyings, *mishkevey*, is a biblically rare word also used in Genesis 49:4 to describe the heterosexual incest of Jacob's son, Reuben, with Jacob's concubine. It is used only in Genesis 49:4, Leviticus 18:22, Leviticus 20:13. It is a plural-looking form of *mishkav*, but rather than indicating a multiple, mishkevey adjusts the meaning of mishkav slightly; to wit, Genesis 49:4 reveals that *lyings* describe a bed, a couch, and metaphorically sexual intercourse. The meaning of the plural form differs from the meaning of the singular form. In English, such a switch in meaning may occur in a plural-like form as well.

---

[30] Lings, K Renato. 2009. "The 'Lyings' of a Woman: Male-Male Incest in Leviticus 18.22?" Theology & Sexuality 15.2 (2009): 231. doi:10.1558/tse. v15i2.231. The parentheses indicate words supplied to smooth the flow of meaning.

[31] In agreeing with Lings, I propose that ancient rabbis adjusted their interpretation of these words to accommodate their nationalistic prejudices. Scroggs agrees with Lings in the former's discussion of how rabbis adjusted their interpretation of the Hebrew in Leviticus 20:13. Robin Scroggs. *The New Testament and Homosexuality,* (Philadelphia, PA: Fortress Press, 1983), Kindle edition, "Stern Opposition–Rabbinic Terminology for Male Homosexuality."

Manner, the way things happen, differs from manners, the way polite society wishes behavior to happen. We again see such a meaning change in the word air. Air indicates atmosphere. Airs denote a show of false grandeur. The word good becomes goods in the plural form and changes its sense.

By using lyings, Jacob emphasizes something different than the sex act. The words condemn Rueben's character as womanly because of his incest. Incest rather than same-sex intercourse is the direct literary link to the act forbidden by Leviticus 18:22.

The topic of Leviticus 18 is incest and related acts that damage the family unit. Leviticus 18 deals with the prohibition of incestuous sin. In Leviticus 18:6, it is the "close relative" (ESV) who comes into view and remains the focus, at least through verse 18. Most of the chapter forbids incestuous transgressions against a female. The place of 18:22 is to make incest with a male equally wrong. The placement of same-sex incest near the end of the prohibitions provides the discourse with a balanced conclusion by extending protection to female and male family members. Lings' translation makes sense as a conclusion to the Leviticus 18 sin list.

Lings' translation makes sense of the chapter's organization. Lings' insights unify Chapter 18 around threats to the family by continuing a focus on incest. The entire pericope of verses 6-23 track with the theme of the sanctity of home life. Avoiding incest is a vital part of a happy home. Leviticus chapters 17-27 address the path of goodness, the calling of Israel to be holy like God. The chapters advocate "regulating sexual behavior [to the intent of] ... the safeguarding and preservation of the marital context in which sexual acts are to occur."[32] Home life needs protecting.

---

[32] Grenz, *Welcoming but Not Affirming*, 40.

Steven E. Eike

This safeguarding can be seen to extend through verse 23. Verse 19, for instance, anticipates that most women will not travel from home during menstruation. The next verse prohibits coitus with a neighbor's wife in near proximity to family doings, "just over the back fence," as it were. In that menstruating time, when the neighbor's wife is free from fear of impregnation, a male neighbor must not approach her with sexual intent. Clearly, the giving of a child to burn in the arms of Molech (18:22) violates the nurturing family.

The prohibitions bear a strong relationship to maintaining a safe space in the home. God wants a joyful home. Incest with a partner of either sex would mutilate the refuge of the home in opposition to God's intent of joy (18:5). Gordon Wenham translates verse five, "You must keep my rules and my laws. If a man does them, he will enjoy life through them: I am the Lord."[33] God created humans to enjoy his way. The proscriptions of Leviticus 18 and 20 follow the Lord's appeal that Israel must not follow the damaging ways of the nation of Egypt or Canaan. Apparently, the ways of Canaan were unfavorable to the joyful life. The writer lists family-related offenses that damage the home. The remainder of the chapter urges Israel's compliance to God's way as opposed to the ways of the lands he would drive out before them so that their experience in the land is not bitter.

Leviticus 18 and 20 respond to the need of women, in particular for protection. In ancient historical context, the term *woman* was derisive. Biblical history offers evidence of common abuse of women that the many worldviews of the time permitted

---

[33] Gordon J. Wenham, *The Book of Leviticus* in The New International Commentary on the Old Testament (Grand Rapids, MI: William B. Eerdmans, 1979), 248.

and even encouraged. Women as a group were not considered valuable in the ancient Middle East. For example, Lot offered his daughters for mob rape rather than suffer the indignity upon his male visitors (Gen. 19:8), and Abraham chanced his wife to Abimelech to protect his own neck (Gen 20:2). These aggressions opposed God's will. Such is the power of a culturally acquired worldview.

God, in Leviticus 18 and 20, set a high moral standard for the day. Womanhood was not respected in ancient times. Archeological research confirms the low status of women. Janet Monge and Page Selinsky investigated violence against women in the Iron Age period (c. 800 BCE) in the Iranian town of Hasanlu. Through skeletal analysis, they determined "a sub-portion of face fractures are the result of accidental violence in both males and females, while the remaining and significant portion in females is associated with interpersonal violence directed specifically against females."[34] Therefore, if the experience in Hasanlu may be generalized, the degrading of women continued many years after Genesis. As Monge and Selinsky report, "It would appear that women in this region of the Near East (Iranian plateau) led lives subject to abuse or injury, in addition to the risk of violent death at the hands of enemies (fulfilled at Hasanlu c.800 BCE [sic])."[35] The study suggests that the abuse fell uniquely on women.

---

[34] Janet Monge and Page Selinsky, "Patterns of violence against women in the Iron Age town of Hasanlu, Solduz Valley, Iran Women in Antiquity" in *Women in Antiquity: Real Women across the Ancient World*, ed. Stephanie Lynn Budin and Jean Macintosh Turfa (London: Routledge, 2016) 147.
[35] Ibid.

Aristotle (384-322 BCE) held misogynist concepts of women. His teacher Plato assumed that "less rational souls were reincarnated as women."[36] Aristotle considered women to be malformed men, "Just as it sometimes happens that deformed [Mutilated is an alternate translation.] offspring are produced by deformed parents ... the female is as it were a deformed male; ... [lacking] one constituent, and one only, the principle of Soul [the ability to reason and sense correctly]."[37] Aristotle believed females contributed no soul to their offspring. Only males transmitted soul through semen.[38] Therefore, only the male contributed the soul of a child. The practical display of such soulless deviancy was thought to be emotions that quenched reason in all areas but homemaking. DeFranza summarizes Aristotle, "Aristotle [reasoned] ... from particulars to universals. The weakness of women's bodies was taken as evidence of the weakness of women's souls. And since the soul is the form [the immortal concept behind all that is physical] of the body and the seat of reason, women's lesser bodily strength was assumed to correspond with lesser strength of soul or mind."[39]

Studying the late Roman period, Mathew Kuefler found women's character to be stereotyped as "carnal, irrational, voluptuous, fickle, manipulative, and deceitful."[40] Scholar Kathryn

---

[36] Aristotle, *Generation of Animals*, trans. A. L. Peck, (Cambridge, MA: Harvard University Press, 2014), 175.

[37] Ibid.

[38] Nicholas D. Smith, "Plato and Aristotle on the Nature of Women." *Journal of the History of Philosophy* 21, no. 4 (1983): 477.

[39] DeFranza, *Sex Difference in Christian Theology*, Kindle edition, 112.

[40] Mathew Kuefler, *The Manly Eunuch* the Chicago Series on Sexuality, History and Society ed. John C. Fout (Chicago, IL: University of Chicago Press, 2001), 35.

Ringrose says of women's status in the Byzantine world between the sixth and twelfth centuries CE, "Women were assumed to lack the ability to control their physical, emotional, or sexual appetites."[41] History reveals the degrading of women's character for a period of over 2,000 years in the near-east. These examples demonstrate that ancient Middle Eastern culture considered women to be vastly inferior humans. To be called a woman was to be labeled characterless and depraved, exactly the descriptor to fit Reuben and the violators of Leviticus 18 and 20.

The historical degradation of the female sex suggests a case can be made for *woman* to have been a slighting term like "sissy" today but much worse. Jacob called Reuben a woman: in the parlance of his day, an inferior, a manipulator, and a moral weakling. Jacob declared Reuben had lowered himself to the level of an unethical conniver like the ancient stereotype of any female. The "lyings of a woman" refers to the illicit sexual pursuits of a very unprincipled person. The meaning of Leviticus 18:22 becomes clear. God's people "shall not lie woman lyings." God declares his opposition to incest and, by extension, any sexual expression that is especially damaging within the family circle, whether acted out toward either females or males. What is also clear is that selfless, same-sex love and marriage are outside the scope of Leviticus 18.

---

[41] Kathryn M. Ringrose, *The Perfect Eunuchs and the Social Construction of Gender in Byzantium*, (Chicago, IL: University of Chicago Press, 2004), 36.

Leviticus 20:13

Leviticus 20 reads like a commentary on Leviticus 18. It reorders the list in 18 and assigns ultimate penalties to violating its prohibitions. Oriented against incestuous living, it repeats most of the forbidden acts of the earlier chapter. With respect to same-sex eroticism, chapter 20 again uses lyings, mishkevey, in the word's only biblical context, incest.

Mishkevey incest is no more abominable than any other home-damaging deed. In Chapter 20, the penalties for violating the family circle are equal and ultimate in nature. Interestingly, the Scripture records no occasion at which the death penalty is applied. Verse 13, which prohibits incestuous behavior toward either sex, receives no greater penalty than other home-breaking sins.

The prohibition of Molech worship receives considerable attention at the fore. Although the practices of Molech worship are not well known, incestual transgressions were linkable with Molech worship in the minds of the lawgiver. John E. Hartley urges the laws against offering children to Molech [in particular] reveal that children are not to be treated as objects that may be used at a parents [sic] desire or as expendable in order to move the divine world to answer the anxieties and whims of their parents.[42]

The prioritized listing condemning Molech worship suggests that the land God assigned for Israel to conquer was rife with Molech-based incest, child sacrifice, and family abuse. It is no

---

[42] John E. Hartley, *Leviticus,* vol. 4 of Word Biblical Commentary, (Grand Rapids, MI: Zondervan Academic, 1992) Kindle edition, 299.

wonder God assigned that society to destruction. As with the Nazi genocide, one may wonder why God did not acted earlier but delayed 400 years. The full answer may be beyond human reasoning. God would have acted with mercy throughout.

The doings within a family compose the sphere of Leviticus 18 and 20. God prioritizes the health of families. Little people are not little or lesser to God. Women are not inferiors. All members must be respected and protected within the family unit. Neither Leviticus 18 nor Leviticus 20 addresses same-sex activity outside the family limits. Neither chapter limits marriage to heterosexual partners.

Associated Passages: Deuteronomy 23:17-18 and Judges 19

There must never be a sacred prostitute among the young women of Israel nor a sacred male prostitute among the young men of Israel. You must never bring the pay of a female prostitute or the wage of a male prostitute into the temple of the Lord your God in fulfillment of any vow, for both of these are abhorrent to the Lord your God. Deut 23: 17-18 (NET)

They were having a good time, when suddenly some men of the city, some good-for-nothings, surrounded the house and kept beating on the door. They said to the old man who owned the house, "Send out the man who came to visit you so we can take carnal knowledge of him." The man who owned the house went outside and said to them, "No, my brothers! Don't do this wicked thing! After all, this man is a guest in my house. Don't do such a disgraceful thing! Here are my virgin daughter and my guest's concubine. Judges 19: 17-24

Though the above verses are sometimes used to condemn same-sex activity, they respectively describe prostitution in religious worship and gang rape like that in the Sodom incident of Genesis 19. Their message does not impact the issue of same-sex preference. The Deuteronomy passage plainly deals with the senselessness of paying a vow to Yahweh with earnings from shrine prostitution. The second, from Judges, records an expansion of Gentile sin into the Jewish world. In Judges 19 is seen as a shameful deed of regional pride like that, narrated in Genesis 19, except that now it is Israelites who are the evildoers, as Scroggs notes.[43] Inhibition of same-sex monogamy has no part either in Deuteronomy 23:17-18 or Judges 19.

---

[43] Scroggs. *The New Testament and Homosexuality*, Kindle edition, "Palestinian Judaism: Stern Opposition–The Torah."

Summary of the Law on Same-sex Marriage

A look back at the Law recalls the following:

- The Old Testament Law does not categorize same-sex attraction as a sin.
- A literal-contextual translation from the Hebrew Masoretic Text of Leviticus 18:22 and 29:13 limits its application to incestuous same-sex activity.
- The term *woman,* as in Leviticus 18 and 20, was derisive. To be called a woman in ancient times was to be labeled characterless and depraved, exactly the descriptor to fit Reuben, who committed incest with his father's concubine (Gen 49:4) and the incestuous persons of Leviticus 18 and 20.
- A loving, same-sex marriage is not a subject of the Hebrew Scriptures.

SUMMARY OF THE OLD TESTAMENT ON SAME-SEX MARRIAGE

The Old Testament case against same-sex marriage falls well short of the facts. The Yahwist and the Pentateuch harmonize, but not by declaring [homo] sexual practices to be abhorrent, as Gagnon proposes; quite the opposite. Hebrew Scripture's unity clears the way to understand legitimate homosexual marriage.[44] Adam expresses delight only in his similarity to Eve. He makes no comment about anatomical differences. The Sodom story illustrates the outcome of pride, not the evil of same-sex attraction. The sin of Ham has no bearing on like-sex attraction issues. The Law condemns homosexuality only if it is incest. Arguments against same-sex unions using the Old Testament fall short.

---

[44] Gagnon, *The Bible and Homosexual Practice*, ch. 1-IV.

SAME-SEX MARRIAGE IN
THE NEW TESTAMENT

The New Testament builds on the platform of the Old rather than contradicts it. Christian scholars agree. Jesus agrees. Walter Elwell identifies Jesus' understanding of the Hebrew canon, "The Old Testament was the Word of God, and its authority was not open to dispute." Ewell observes, "Most frequently, he [Jesus] would quote from the Old Testament when he wanted to make a point."[45] Contemporary Old Testament theologian John Walton shares reverence for Hebrew Bible, "By his teaching, Jesus not only certified the continuing authority of the Old Testament law but also clarified and illuminated what had been implicit regarding human intent and motives."[46] Luke affirms Jesus' high view of the leading of the Scriptures. On the

---

[45] Walter A. Elwell and Robert W. Yarbrough, *Encountering the New Testament: A Historical and Theological Survey*, 3rd ed. in Encountering Biblical Studies (Grand Rapids, MI: Baker Publishing Group, 2013), Kindle edition, "Lord, Teach Us –The Form of Jesus's Message."

[46] Andrew E. Hill; John H. Walton. A Survey of the Old Testament (p. 71). Zondervan Academic. Kindle Edition.

Emmaus Road, he explained, "Beginning with Moses and all the Prophets, he explained... what was said in all the Scriptures concerning himself." Luke 24:27 The Old Testament was the standard of truth for Paul. Peter Balla summarizes Paul's teaching of Scripture's authority, "In all the cases when Paul quotes the O.T., he does so in order to support what he is saying with an authoritative text."[47] This Scripture, which both Jesus and Paul declared reliable, shows no fault in same-sex union, the New Testament would have a very high hill to climb to reverse the testimony of the Old. Indeed, a reversal is impossible for those of evangelical faith.

Christ's followers must, therefore, build upon the Hebrew message that accepts same-gender relationships. The alternative is that God changed the template for sin for reasons unrevealed and, at the same time, perjured his divine word. Yet, "God is not human, that he should lie, not a human being, that he should change his mind." Num 23:19 God "does not change like shifting shadows." James 1:17 Yahweh's ethics remain consistent. How, then, did the typical evangelical New Testament interpretation go wrong?

---

[47] Peter Balla, "2 Corinthians" in *Commentary on the New Testament Use of the Old Testament*, ed. G. K. Beale and D. A. Carson, (Grand Rapids, MI: Baker Academic, 2017), Kindle edition, 753.

Cultural Pressures Twisted First Century Worldviews Of Many

To begin, we "put... [ourselves] into the frame of mind of those to whom they [Paul's letters] were addressed," as Tom Wright says.[48] We seek to sense the worldview of first-century people as much as possible: the basic attitudes and actions affirmed by their culture. It has often been said that the Bible was written for us but not to us. Paul communicated for the ears of his time, first-century ears. They were his audience, and he knew them. We want to know how the first century would hear and interpret Paul's intent, then we can apply that intent to the present day. Consequently, we will look briefly at the societal influences of first-century times.

---

[48] N. T. Wright, *Paul and the Faithfulness of God: Two Book Set (Christian Origins and the Question of God 4)*. Fortress Press: Minneapolis, MN, Kindle Edition Preface.

Jews Of The Time Largely Held A Biased Worldview Against Gentiles

The Historical Development

Judaism crusaded against Gentile ways during the Second Temple period. Gentile nations had conquered Judah and were threatening Hebrew culture. Devout Jews reacted with fear. Instead of loving others, Israel conceived a narrative that represented their nation as good and Gentiles as evil. Such nationalism began to ease God out of the picture. Even the knowledgeable priest Ezra buckled to the pressure of nationalism and fear. He yielded to a mistaken fear of God's judgment upon Israel because some had taken pagan wives. The pressures on Ezra were internal: social, undiscerningly literal, and political. Under pressure, Ezra should not have accepted the advice of a prominent advisor, Shekaniah. Shekaniah, son of Jehiel, advocated that the trespassers abandon their foreign family. Ezra 10:1–5 Ezra commanded the erring Hebrews to divorce their wives and abandon their children. As a consequence, he ignored the prophet Malachi's words from half a century earlier. Malachi had proclaimed the heart of God concerning divorce, "The man who hates and divorces his wife, says the Lord, the God of Israel, does violence to the one he should protect." Mal 2:16

Shaye Cohen believes Ezra acted out of trauma, the trauma of Babylon's horrific devastation of Jerusalem, and the demise of political and religious hopes for a Hebrew kingdom. In a panic, Ezra reacted against the outward to, as it were, "make the problem go away." Fear had entered Ezra's religion and caused his worldview to evolve against God's love. As much as we may empathize with Ezra's error, it was tragic. It was against God. He fell when he should have stood.

The Bible's review of Ezra's contemporary, Nehemiah, the governor, makes no mention of fear in him. In the mid to late fifth century BCE, faced the same situation of racial intermarriage as Ezra; Scripture does not report that Nehemiah ordered divorce. Nehemiah reflects instead,

> I rebuked them [those who had intermarried with a Gentile] and called curses down on them. I beat some of the men and pulled out their hair. I made them take an oath in God's name and said: "You are not to give your daughters in marriage to their sons, nor are you to take their daughters in marriage for your sons or for yourselves." Nehemiah 13:25

Whatever may be said about Nehemiah's methods, he knew the importance of a spiritually united community, and in the spirit of Malachi, he sought to protect the future by not ruining families in the present.

But, in this case, right does not prevail among the Hebrews. Nehemiah did right, but Ezra had fame and the people's hearts. Ezra owned the power of influence. "Josephus (*Antiq.* XI, 183 [v. 8]) relates concerning Ezra that it was his [grand] fate, after being honored by the people, to die an old man and be buried with great magnificence in Jerusalem."[49] Ezra's influence could not

---

[49] Edwin M. Yamauchi, "Ezra–Nehemiah" in *The Expositor's Bible Commentary*, ed. Frank E. Gaebelein, (Grand Rapids, MI: Zonderevan, 1977), 589.

help but reinforce bias against Gentiles within the Jewish community; a bias that would show in ways that include condemning any and all same-sex relationships. Equally ominous, Ezra set a precedent for ignoring select bits of God's revelation.[50]

Aristeas, writing roughly three centuries after Ezra's time, slandered Gentile sexuality. Ezra's error had lived on. Nationalism, civil religion, had become an interpretative method. It had become culturally acceptable to hold a pre-existing bias against Gentile sex practices.[51] In addition, Aristeas put an indefensibly positive light on Jewish culture. Gagnon summarizes though he wrongly considers it evidence against same-sex relations of any type, "The author [Aristeas] tells us that Jews are morally superior to the gentiles [sic] in that the latter 'not only draw near to (or: procure) males but also defile their mothers and even their daughters. We [Jews] are quite separated from these practices."[52] Gagnon should recognize that Aristeas' letter shows an untenable partiality toward the Hebrews. The moral tone of Aristeas is unrealistic. Contra Aristeas, Paul wrote Romans 2:1 to convince Jews that their behavior was just as bad as the Gentiles.

---

[50] "The Jewish *aggadah* [a significant piece of Jewish tradition] regarded Ezra with great honor. He was not just a priest but the high priest and a second Moses. He was especially revered for restoring the Law of Moses, which had been forgotten, and for establishing the regular public reading of the Law. He is also credited with setting up schools for the study of the Law." John Van Seters, "Ezra." In *Encyclopedia of Religion*, 2nd ed., edited by Lindsay Jones, 2946-2947. Vol. 5. Detroit, MI: Macmillan Reference U.S.A., 2005. *Gale eBooks*

[51] Aristeas' place in history derives from his retrospective report on the translation of the Hebrew Bible into Greek that began about 250 BCE.

[52] Gagnon, *The Bible and Homosexual Practice*, ch. 1-IV. Kindle edition. 3327 of 10277

Aristeas' lack of realism confirms Jewish prejudice and, at the same time, compromises his objectivity to object against same-sex relationships.

The Jewish philosopher Philo (20 B.C.E.–C.E. 45) embodied the nurtured prejudice against Gentile behavior of the common Jewish worldview. Philo was an influential writer from Alexandria, Egypt, whose life overlapped that of Jesus. Of Philo, Gagnon says, "For Philo and Josephus, homosexual conduct was merely the most outrageous example of a much wider range of sinful excess."[53] Gagnon expresses, "Early Judaism was unanimous in its rejection of homosexual conduct. We are unaware of any dissenting voices. The data comes primarily from Philo and Josephus."[54] But the worldviews of both Philo and Josephus were twisted by their culture. Philo held to a 1st-century Jewish cultural view that intercourse that cannot produce offspring is wrong because it cannot lead to childbearing. Philo believed, "Male sperm is life itself, so the wasting of it in intercourse with other males is regarded as a serious offense."[55] James Brownson sums up the central point of this view of Philo, "For Philo, this linkage between sex and procreation is definitive, and it shapes all that he has to say about sex."[56] Philo's view has no biblical basis. Indeed, Paul, in his epistles, recognizes sexual obligations to one's marriage partner without qualification. 1 Cor 7:5 Gagnon speculates that Philo's worldview interprets the command of

---

53 Ibid, 1379 of 10277.

54 Ibid, 3319 of 10277.

55 Ibid, 1916 of 10277

56 Brownson, *Bible, Gender, Sexuality,* 239.

Genesis 1:28, "Be fruitful and multiply."[57] But a quick review shows that Genesis 1:28 presents a positive command, not a prohibition. It neither explicitly condemns intercourse with an unfertile woman nor same-sex relations.

Reproduction is essential for survival, but Genesis looks for greater fruitfulness than physical reproduction. The Earth is full. Augustine thought people had filled the earth by the time of Christ. He saw more importance in greater spiritual fruitfulness rather than a larger population.[58] Same-sex couples can produce this better fruit, the fruit of loving God and loving others. Jesus held up such love as God's greatest desire for people. Matt 22:34-40 Philo may be a reliable witness to the worldview of his own Jewish culture. Nevertheless, we must conclude that Philo's witness in same-sex matters should be considered unreliable because he limited his thinking to conform to his culture's prejudice against same-sex relationships.

Josephus's worldview also manifests the deluding power of cultural bias. The Jewish historian Josephus spoke for many Jews when he said: "What are our marriage laws? The Law recognizes no sexual connections, except the natural [kata phusin] union of man and wife, and that only for the procreation of children."[59] Culture can press even the educated, like Josephus and Philo, into its mold. Josephus was a Pharisee of the priestly line and a

---

[57] Gagnon, Robert A. J. The Bible and Homosexual Practice. Abingdon Press. Kindle Edition. 1911 of 10277

[58] Zondervan, Two Views on Homosexuality, the Bible, and the Church (Counterpoints: Bible and Theology) (p. 155). Zondervan Academic. Kindle Edition.

[59] James V. Brownson, *Bible, Gender, Sexuality* (Grand Rapids, MI: Wm. B. Eerdmans Publishing Co.), Kindle edition. 238.

Jewish historian of first-century times. Like Philo, Josephus (ca. C.E. 37–ca. 100) illuminates a first-century Jewish worldview regarding same-sex relationships. Scroggs shows Josephus' biased view of Jewish ethics in his twisting of the story of the Levite and his concubine from Judges 19-21.

> Josephus [reports Scroggs] ... tells the story in a way illuminating his prejudices (Ant. V. 136-49). To him, fellow Israelites cannot be portrayed as having homosexual desires; hence the Benjamites, the Hebrew villains of the story, lust only for the concubine, not for the man, as the text reports. Indeed, they actively seize the woman from the house (143-46), also contrary to the narrative in Judges. In this way, Josephus removes any hint of homosexuality from the story.[60]

In Aristeas', Philo's, and Josephus' worlds, their bias against Gentiles warped into a narrative that same-sex activity was the dangerous province of non-Jews but never occurred among Jews. These three ancients witness to the distorted worldview of their day cannot reliably witness to a biblical worldview of sexuality.

But Gentile Rome was more influenced by Greek culture than by Hebrew culture. Not all of Paul's audience would be intimately affected by the prejudice of Jewish writers, but the prejudices held by the Greek philosophers and the patriarchal ideal of Greeks were passed down to Rome. Twenty-first-century

---

[60] Robin Scroggs. The New Testament and Homosexuality (Kindle Locations 1001-1003). Kindle Edition.

Christian leaders largely fail to understand either the first-century Jew's racism or the elite Roman's abusive sexual practices that plagued and polarized Paul's hearers. The public culture of Paul's Jewish and Gentile audience was awash with prejudice and abuse.

An Abusive Roman Upper Class

The worldview of first-century Rome was set in the context of classism, with upper-class males satisfied in their debauched pattern of behavior. Wealthy Roman men warped the first century's worldview to their advantage. They had the power to subjugate the lower classes to their will. Aristocrats ruled, wrote, and kept all Roman records. Scroggs noted the imbalance in public records of the day, excepting Paul's writings, "What is known about women and the lower classes is filtered through the perspectives and prejudices of this privileged group."[61] Paul urged Christians to distance themselves from the Empire's worldview for their own temporal and eternal good. 1 Cor 3:18-20 The Empire's aristocracy left the world of inter-sex and homosexually formed individuals to be shuffled away from relevancy somewhere near to the women. DeFranza writes of the history in modern terms this way,

> In the classical world, sex and gender were understood as a ladder of ascent toward perfection. At the top were manly men—understood as the pinnacle of both male and human perfection. At the bottom were women and children. Unmanly men, hermaphrodites, and eunuchs occupied the middle.[62]

---

[61] Robin Scroggs. The New Testament and Homosexuality (Kindle Location 239). Kindle Edition.

[62] Megan K. DeFranza, *Sex Difference in Christian Theology*. (Grand Rapids, Michigan: Wm. B. Eerdmans Publishing Co., 2015), Kindle edition, 114.

Using Foucault's research, Amy Richlin reports the shame of this middle group, "The social misery that must have awaited any adult passive male, and moral condemnations of anal and oral intercourse are two a penny."[63] High-class men considered either penetration of women or boys a normal mode of sexual expression. "At the same time, the lowest form of abnormal adult male sex activity was passivity, allowing oneself to be penetrated."[64]

Passivity in men and boys signaled perversion and humiliation to Rome's upper crust. "Their class consciousness equated sexual submission with loss of honor, admission of inferiority, and lack of virility."[65] Similarly, the quality of gentleness was used as an accusation. So Tacitus describes how Valerius Asiaticus, when accused of female softness, used a Roman worldview to justify himself and shame his prosecutor by responding, "Ask your sons, Suillius, they'll testify that I'm a man."[66] In other words, Valerius intimated that he had used Suillius' sons sexually. In an ancient political tract, a Pseudo-Cicero is said to have responded to his adversary, "As for what you insinuated against my youth... I think I am as far from *impudicitia* [here meaning receiving anal penetration] as you are from *pudicitia* [here meaning not receiving anal penetration]."[67] In Roman culture, as Richlin puts it, "A passive sexual subculture would have been marked off

---

[63] Amy Richlin, "Not before Homosexuality: The Materiality of the Cinaedus and the Roman Law against Love between Men." *Journal of the History of Sexuality* 3, no. 4 (1993): 528.

[64] Amy Richlin, "Not before Homosexuality", 533.

[65] Ibid, 535.

[66] Ibid, 538.

[67] Ibid.

[among other ways]... by loathing."[68] The Roman elite despised those who violated the perverse sexual norms of their worldview. Paul evaluated the Roman take on sexuality as abusive.

The threat of the upper class's power to abuse and also to kidnap family members surely worried Christians. Christians knew the poor and the slaves were the erotic playgrounds of the upper class. Rome's habits threatened the Christian stance on marital fidelity as well. John Boswell quotes the Roman writer Suetonius (c. 69 – c. 130/140 CE),

> Wives [of the higher class] often encouraged husbands to employ slaves (of either gender) for sexual release, and the attitude of Antony on the subject of heterosexual relations is probably typical of Roman males. In a letter to Augustus (who, like Antony himself, was married at the time) he asked, "Can it matter where or in whom you put it?[69]

Elite Romans practiced dehumanizing objectification with impunity. Plutarch (ca. 45–120 CE) saw virtue in taking full advantage of the beautiful, "The noble lover of beauty engages in love wherever he sees excellence and splendid natural endowment without regard for any difference in physiological detail."[70] Naturally, male prostitution was an active business. In the first

---

[68] Ibid, 554.

[69] John Boswell, *Christianity, Social Tolerance, and Homosexuality: Gay People in Western Europe from the Beginning of the Christian Era to the Fourteenth Century.* Chicago: University of Chicago Press, 1981, 62.

[70] Matthew Vines, *God and the Gay Christian: The Biblical Case in Support of Same-Sex Relationships.* First Ed. New York: Convergent Books, 2014, 33.

century, male prostitutes were legal.[71] At the same time, traffickers, well-healed and high-born, all threatened the children of the slaves and those of low-class station. Michel Foucault characterized the Roman mindset about sex, "love for boys was practiced for the most part with young slaves, about whose status there was no reason to worry,"[72] but victims even included the free-born.[73] Artemidorus, in his second-century C.E. book, *The Interpretation of Dreams*, wrote, "The sex of the partner makes little difference of course; girl or boy, what matters is that one is dealing with a slave," a piece of property.[74]

To the Roman elite, the image of God did not exist in a slave. Yet for Christians, God's image in every person was an essential truth, sexual purity was a childhood right, and marital unity was not to be violated. Consequently, fear of sexual predators must have horrified Christians in Paul's day.

---

[71] Thomas A. J. McGinn, *Prostitution, Sexuality, and the Law in Ancient Rome* New York: Oxford University Press, 1998, 268.

[72] Michel, Foucault and Robert Hurley. *The History of Sexuality,* First Vintage books edition, New York, NY: Vintage Books, 1988, 181.

[73] John Boswell, *Christianity, Social Tolerance, and Homosexuality,* 57.

[74] Michel, Foucault and Robert Hurley. *The History of Sexuality,* 24.

Steven E. Eike

The Influence of Sexually Perverse Emperors

According to ancient sources, in Apostle Paul's lifetime the Roman emperors' sexual excesses worsened. Gaius Suetonius Tranquillus (70 C.E. after 122), a Roman historian of twelve Caesars, reports that both Caesar Augustus and his predecessor Julius Caesar "allowed themselves to be penetrated anally and orally by other adult men."[75] About Augustus' successor, Tiberius, "people said that he trained boys in their earliest youth... whom he called 'fishies'... to busy themselves between his thighs as he was swimming."[76] Further, Suetonius wrote, "He became notorious because of a still greater and more shameful reputation for disgraceful conduct, behavior that may not be appropriate to be discussed or heard, much less believed."[77] Emperor Gaius Caligula (ruled A.D. 37-41) succeeded Tiberius. A study of Caligula's marriages led Marleen Flory to diagnose his nature as "tyrannical and capricious."[78] Among her examples, she cites how while eating with a woman and her fiancé, who were to be married that day, Caligula addressed the man saying, "Do not fondle my wife." He then took her away, married her for a few days, and subsequently both divorced and deported her.

---

[75] Masterson, *Making Manhood Hard* Tiberius and Latin literary representations of erectile dysfunction Judith P. Hallett [Sex in Antiquity: Exploring Gender and Sexuality in the Ancient World] 417.

[76] Amy Richlin, *Reading Boy-Love And Child-Love In The Greco-Roman World*, [.Sex in Antiquity: Exploring Gender and Sexuality in the Ancient World] Masterson, 360.

[77] Masterson *Making Manhood Hard*, 409

[78] Flory, Marleen Boudreau. "Caligula's "Inverecundia": A Note on Dio Cassius 59.12.1." *Hermes* 114, no. 3 (1986): 365-71. Accessed January 2, 2021. http://www.jstor.org/stable/4476511. 369.

Suetonius wrote, "Besides his incest with his sisters and his notorious passion for Pyrallis, the prostitute, there was hardly any lady of distinction with whom he did not make free."[79]

> Caligula would invite upper-class women with their husbands to supper, and as they passed by the couch on which he reclined at the table, examine them very closely, like those who traffic in slaves; and if anyone from modesty held down her face, he raised it up with his hand. Afterward, as often as he was in the humor, he would quit the room, send for her he liked best, and in a short time return with marks of recent disorder about them.[80]

Philo summed up Caligula's character from a Jew's point of view, "this hater of the citizens, this devourer of the people, this pestilence, this destructive evil, began to banish all the seeds of peace from his country."[81] Gaius Caligula was assassinated with multiple stabs into his genitals by his security force, including a military man whom he had sexually used.

---

[79] Suetonius. The Lives of the Twelve Caesars, public domain, Caius Caesar Caligula, XXXVII.

[80] Ibid.

[81] The Works of Philo On The Embassy To Gaius, XV.108
http://www.earlychristianwritings.com/yonge/book40.html

PAUL WROTE FROM GOD'S WORLDVIEW

P aul's worldview conflicted with civil religion. As a learned and devoted Jew of the day, Paul thought, lived, and wrote in opposition to the excesses of Rome and its emperors. His early life exposed him to two villains of the Empire: Tiberius and his successor, Gaius Caligula, who reigned for less than four years. [82] Later in life, he would experience Nero (who ruled A.D. 54–68) firsthand. As a traveler and a scholar of Hebrew ethics, Paul's evaluation of Roman leaders and their effect on society would have been insightful. Of course, he knew God's will as expressed in Jewish teaching. Paul had compassion for people's circumstances. As an apostle and pastor for Christ, his letters pointed toward the way of hope in Jesus. He did not find danger in loving, faithful, same-sex relations. He had a godly worldview.

Three Pauline passages in the New Testament have been used inappropriately to say that Paul denounced homosexuality

---

[82] The Damascus Road incident can be dated within A.D. 32–35. Tiberius' reign finished in his 77th year of age in A.D. 37. Gaius Caligula allegedly murdered him by directive.

in toto and, therefore, same-sex marriage. The earliest such passage is in Paul's first letter to the Corinthian church. The last such passage, in Paul's first letter to Timothy, resembles the first and can be evaluated with it. Additionally, just three or so years after 1 Corinthians and about two years after Nero began to reign, Paul wrote the first chapter of his Letter to the Romans, which has been central to the argument to condemn all same-sex marriage. We shall examine Paul's writings carefully.

Paul Was About Unifying Christians In Love

Paul wrote Romans to unify Jewish and Gentile Christians in love. His introduction tells his purpose. In it, he notes that both groups belong to Jesus, who loves them. Paul writes to them about his love wishes for their grace and peace. (Ro. 1:6-7) In love, he has long desired to visit them. He wants to gift them spiritually.

Paul wants to gift them with love that overcomes racial and cultural prejudices. His letter suggests he knew of the hardship that their conflict between Jewish Christians and Gentile Christians was causing. Their intimacy needed healing. Their emotions did not support each other. As Thich Nhat Hanh wrote, "Our emotional states impact others, especially when we are in an intimate relationship." Christians have family intimacy as brothers and sisters. (1:13) Paul brought the good news of healing and wholeness through Christ to them, healing and wholeness that works by faith and fulfills the promise of "the righteousness of God," good, all-around peace and health. In Paul's good news, faith would conquer prejudice and restore health to the broken body of Christ.

He goes on to express his concern about the prejudiced mindset of Christian Jews, but without informing them that they are his focus. The Jews blame only Gentiles. But writes Paul, God reveals wrath against all unbelief, and the Jews carried the burdens of unbelief though they did not know it.

Paul begins his letter to the Roman Christians to heal a racial and religious divide. He would have no reason to introduce a racial discrimination discussion but then turn the body of the letter quickly off his subject to gender and sexuality matters. Why would a schooled writer like Paul do such a thing? Close examination shows that Paul's purpose in this passage was not to examine sex roles.

Steven E. Eike

Paul Was Not Examining Sex Roles
In Romans 1:16 - 2:29

Paul's purpose in this passage was not to examine sex roles. He wrote Romans 1:16–2:29 to goad Jewish Christian hearers into acknowledging they have no moral high ground above Gentile Christians. To enlighten his fellow Jews, he sets a trap that he will spring later in Chapter 2. He wants to break through their hardness to the Gentiles so the Roman Hebrews will love all humankind. Gentiles alone did not create earth's problems.

Some Jews felt God had abandoned the Gentiles. Therefore, they thought Gentiles, being without God's help, dishonored their bodies and behaved as if debauched. Romans 1:18–20, 23-27 Jews regarded themselves as the Gentiles' superiors. Paul saw hypocrisy in supposing their race and culture had made them morally superior. Jews needed to accept the Gentiles as cherished by God, who created all in the divine image. Paul provoked their pride to a peak to catch them in their attitude of disrespect. He concludes by saying in Romans 2:1, "You, therefore, have no excuse, you who pass judgment on someone else, for at whatever point you judge another, you are condemning yourself because you who pass judgment do the same things."

Romans does not condemn same-sex erotic relationships. Having dismissed any centrality of gender roles from the force of Paul's discussion in Romans 1, we examine the place of same-sex marriage in the remainder of Romans.

Same-sex marriage detractors center their criticisms in Romans around 1:20–32. In this passage, Paul condemns anyone, Jew or Gentile, who with knowledge of God's glory, rejects

God's path of love to follow profligate desires. In response, God lets them experience the result of their foolishness, a life of self-destructive sex which they pursue to their peril. The N.I.V. calls it giving them over in the sinful desires of their hearts to sexual impurity for the degrading of their bodies with one another.

To understand what Paul meant by sexual impurity, we must know how Roman Christians would have defined sexual impurity and also what they considered to be degrading of the body. In Rome, no better example of such sexual perversity existed than Emperor Gaius Caligula of about 15 years before this epistle of Paul. The recent memory of Emperor Caligula would recall his horrifying deeds. Brownson suggests, "Paul's allusion to the emperor can be understood as an indictment of the Gentile world through the behavior of its leaders."[83] Jewish and Gentile Christians would agree that Caligula's sexuality had been vile. As well, Roman elites practiced pederasty, the sexual use of young males, subjugating children for self-pleasuring. Further, adult male-on-male eroticism was considered an acceptable practice of dominance and humiliation.

Tellingly, Roman writings record little about faithful homosexual or lesbian love. Therefore, it would be strange and counterproductive if Paul built his case for Jewish and Gentile moral equality based on a non-issue of the time, selfless same-sex love. Would something nobody thinks about perform Paul's goal of shocking? It was essential to Paul's purpose that Romans 1 raise Jewish objection to a fever so that he could shock them into seeing their guilt. Paul needed genuinely horrifying issues to

---

[83] Brownson, James V. Bible, Gender, Sexuality (p. 159). Wm. B. Eerdmans Publishing Co., Kindle Edition.

Steven E. Eike

outrage the Jewish Christians. A matter of little current moment like genuine same-sex love could not shock. Homosexual love could not have been the issue of Romans 1. There was no shock available there.

Same-sex marriage opponents claim that non-heterosexual eroticism degrades the participant's body. (Ro 1:24) To degrade a body is to treat it in a way that seeks only self-gratification rather than gives God's love and care to another. Today it is called objectifying. Leviticus 19:29 in the Old Testament vilifies objectification, "Do not degrade your daughter by making her a prostitute, or the land will turn to prostitution and be filled with wickedness." The apostle opposes objectification but instead finds value in caring within faithful marital love.

> The husband should fulfill his marital duty to his wife and, likewise, the wife to her husband. The wife does not have authority over her own body but yields it to her husband. In the same way, the husband does not have authority over his own body but yields it to his wife.[84]

Knowing what we do of Rome, we might easily imagine a Roman patriarch cheapening a wife's body, thereby degrading the marriage partnership. Maybe that is why their wives sought extremes of pleasure from other women. Ro 1:18 The reference is most likely to a woman going beyond a husband to seek safe sex in lesbian relationships. Paul disparaged selfish pleasure in male

---

[84] 1 Corinthians 7:3–4

sex activity as well. God's design is to "encourage one another and build each other up."[85] Self-centered sexuality degrades.

The text does not criticize faithful love within either heterosexual or same-sex couples because that kind of love is committed to the best for the other person. Wanton sexuality degrades because it has nothing to give. Paul vilifies the expression of the monstrous ego of the Roman imperial house: prostitution, child abuse, promiscuity, absence of mutuality, and failure of persons to express with their bodies what they say with the rest of their lives. Such persons "receive back the due penalty for their error" in forms of judgment that show the consequence of their misbehavior. Rom. 1: 27[86] Godly love, whether in same-sex or heterosexual partnership, does not degrade.

Nevertheless, with mathematical confidence, some theologians reject the possibility of blessing same-sex marriage. Their reasoning is untrue to God's plan. There is higher ground to occupy in our love for one another. Some of that high ground happens in same-sex marriages. Paul accepts same-sex marriage as another fruitful and loving path.

---

[85] 1 Thessalonians 5:11
[86] Brownson, James V. Bible, Gender, Sexuality (pp. 261-262).

Paul Used Natural (Phusin) To
Mean Generally Expected

The way of the offenders in Romans 1 is called unnatural in the N.I.V. But *phusin*, the word Paul used, means unexpected rather than against God's eternal way. A person wrestling an alligator and winning might seem unnatural in that it is unexpected, but it would not be contrary to the will of God. An interesting story, a legend, illustrates a similarly unnatural event from the Thirty Years' War. Johann Tserclaes, Count of Tilly, led the Catholic armies to victory in city after city-destroying victory. When he reached Rothenberg, he challenged anyone in the city to drink a gallon of wine in a continuous chug to save the town or die. The mayor downed the liquid in one continuous flow. The Count of Tilly left the town in perfect condition. The mayor's feat was unnatural, unexpected, for a man, but not at odds with the will of God for the earth.

Phusin means unexpected. Critics of same-sex marriage often misunderstand *phusin,* which is translated, natural. Romans 1:26-27 reads

> God gave them over to shameful lusts. Even their women exchanged natural sexual relations for unnatural ones. In the same way, the men also abandoned natural relations with women and were inflamed with lust for one another. Men committed shameful acts with other men and received in themselves the due penalty for their error.

We must ask the question, does Paul mean naturally to represent God's objective standard set for all time or usual, anticipated behavior in the time of his writing? To ask the question another way, does 'natural' represent what agrees with God's goal for human existence, or does natural refer to what is expected in some specific culture and place?[87]

Going against Paul's use of phusin, opponents of same-sex eroticism claim it to be an unnatural act at all times and in all places, an action contrary to God's eternal will. They reason that the physical fit of male with female genitalia indicates a Creator's enduringly sole intent. Therefore, to them, departing from heterosexuality is always a sin, missing God's standard. As support, they assume a universal pattern of mammals to propagate heterosexually. After all, they might say no other reproductive option is available, and since propagation is paramount to sustaining the earth, only heterosexual marriage makes sense.

Furthermore, they reason that the great majority of sexual desire in humans is between male and female; therefore, they conclude that only heterosexuality keeps God's purpose. Homosexuality, therefore, must be deviant. Gagnon claims: homosexual eroticism ignores "nature's obvious clues" that God's will is heterosexuality.[88] Therefore only heterosexuality can be God's will.

We will conduct a thorough word study of phusin. The biblical text reveals that the word rendered natural in the New Testament, phusin, denotes a normal expectation of the time.

---

[87] Stanley J. Grenz, *Welcoming but Not Affirming: an Evangelical Response to Homosexuality.* Louisville, KY: Westminster John Knox Press, 1998, 101.
[88] Robert A. J. Gagnon, *The Bible and Homosexual Practice: Texts and Hermeneutics*, (Nashville: Abingdon Press, 2001), Kindle loc. 681 of 10277.

To the Jew, it would not conjure up the idea of an eternal plan of God. Today, we might say that it is natural (phusin) for Aaron Judge to hit home runs. We would not mean that he is out of the will of God if he does not homer. Yet, we expect homers now and again.

The word phusin is in the non-canonical Hebrew history books, *3 Maccabees* and Wisdom, written before the New Testament period. These books that Paul undoubtedly had read reveal phusin to refer to an expectation rather than a God-ordained plan. We even see the reasonableness of phusin as unexpected in a strange mistranslation in *3 Maccabees*. 3:29 R.S.V. It translates phusin as the impossible phrase, *mortal creature."* The author has the enemy of Jews declare, "Every place detected sheltering a Jew is to be made unapproachable and burned with fire, and shall become useless for all time to any *mortal creature.*"[89] Mortal creature is not a synonym for phusin. A more literal translation, using the context, reveals its meaning, normal expectation. The adversary of the Jews wishes the Jew never to have the expected happiness of a home, there.

The Wisdom writer, writing phusin, claims to understand "the natures of animals and the tempers of wild animals."[90] By pairing nature with temper, the author asserts in Hebrew parallelism his familiarity with their behavior. Notice that he does not claim to know these creatures' original or eternal design. Perhaps, God meant animals, like lions, to be peaceful, unlike now. Instead, what does he know? He knows what to expect of them now.

---

[89] *3 Maccabees* (3:29 R.S.V.)
[90] *Wisdom of Solomon*, 7:20.

The writer of *The Wisdom of Solomon* (ca. 50 BCE) uses phusin in 13:1, "All people who were ignorant of God were ignorant by nature." (NRSV) Did God, therefore, design them not to know him? Putting aside potential objections by extreme determinists, God obviously did not. Indeed, the ignorant by nature could be expected to be ignorant of God either due to lack of training or by their own disposition, but not by the design of a good creator. Therefore to the Wisdom writer, nature does not refer to a condition intended by God. Instead, we discover by analysis that phusin refers to what can naturally be expected in the situation of the person not raised under the tutelage of God.

Paul's use of phusis in Romans and beyond confirms Paul's consistent use of phusis to indicate a normal expectation. Observe the first uses in Romans (1:26-27),

> God gave them over to shameful lusts. Even their women exchanged natural [phusin, expected by the culture] sexual relations for unnatural [unexpected or surprising] ones. In the same way, the men also abandoned natural [phusin] relations with women and were inflamed with lust for one another."[91]

Roman society expected temperate behavior from people, so the Roman elite were violating the mores of their community. As Brownson puts it, "Men [of Greco- Roman culture], being overcome by passion, were losing control over their own lives—and

---

[91] Although the N.I.V. uses the term divine nature in 1:20, in Greek, it is but a single word, θειότης, divinity.

thus being subject to shame."[92] Even in evil deeds, Roman society expected men to control themselves fully. Roman culture had its expectations. The people described had abandoned basic societal expectations for violent sexual episodes.

In Romans 2, we find the next use of nature in verse 14, where Paul compliments certain of the Gentiles, "when Gentiles, who do not have the law [the written Hebrew guide of order], do by nature things required by the law, they are a law for themselves." In other words, those who do not have the law may decide to behave in ways of moderation and self-denial that coincide with God's order. Nissinen comments, "Here, the phrase by nature seems to be a way of saying what is in accord with one's own nature or identity rather than a pervasive nature given to all by God—hence the NRSV translation, 'instinctively.'"[93] In other words, some Gentiles possessed an enlightened personal conscience. Some could be expected to behave well.

The word for nature, phusin, is also used in 2:27, although the N.I.V. awkwardly renders it as "physically." "The one who is not circumcised physically [phusin, in the way *expected* by Jews] and yet obeys the law will condemn you who, even though you have the written code and circumcision, are a lawbreaker." Circumcision was their expected but temporary national flag, so to speak. Circumcision had not always been a sign of allegiance with God. It became the temporary, not eternal, symbol of Judaism in the time of Abraham. Before and after the time of the Jewish nation's mission to the world, the sign of following Yahweh was inward: love and obedience to God and love of

---

[92] Brownson, James V. Bible, Gender, Sexuality (p. 201). Wm. B. Eerdmans Publishing Co., Kindle Edition

[93] Brownson, *Bible, Gender, Sexuality*, 226.

others. Circumcision was their expected but temporary national flag, so to speak.

In the N.I.V. chapter 11, Romans features the book's final uses of natural and nature, phusin, in verses 21 and 24,

> For if God did not spare the *natural* branches, he would not spare you either. Consider, therefore, the kindness and sternness of God: sternness to those who fell, but kindness to you, provided that you continue in his kindness. Otherwise, you also will be cut off. And if [Jews] they do not persist in unbelief, they will be grafted in, for God is able to graft them in again. After all, if you were cut out of an olive tree that is wild by *nature* and, contrary to *nature,* were grafted into a cultivated olive tree, how much more readily will these, the natural branches, be grafted into their own olive tree!

Consider the following paraphrase which makes the meaning of phusin come clear.

> For if God did not spare the branches that one would *expect* to be spared, he will not spare you either.... If you, a Gentile, were cut out of an olive tree that is wild like is *expected*, and contrary to expectation were grafted into a cultivated olive tree, how much more readily will these, the branches that one would *expect* to be there, the Jewish people, be grafted into their own olive tree!

Paul has consistently used the word, translated as natural throughout Romans, to picture expected results, not God's inviolable will.

Going beyond Romans, two of Paul's books written chronologically before Romans contain the word phusin: Galatians and 1 Corinthians. Neither book uses phusin, nature or natural, to indicate God's guide to humankind. Both use phusin to indicate a culturally expected behavior.

Paul goes to lengths in his writing to put Jews and Gentiles on the same footing. He wants a blending of Jews and Gentiles as Christ-followers. In Galatians 2:15, Paul referred to his Jewish nature and Peter's, "How is it... that you force Gentiles to follow Jewish customs? We who are Jews by birth [phusin; expectation] and not sinful Gentiles." The Jews could be expected to act like Jews. Paul's rebuke intends to void any eternal status for Jewish tradition. Once again, phusis reflects a behavioral expectation, not an inviolable intent of God's will.

The meaning of phusin shows as an expectation in 1 Corinthians 11:14 as well, "Does not the very nature of things teach you that if a man has long hair, it is a disgrace to him?" Paul was not identifying God's eternal plan for hair since God's Nazarite vow required men to have long hair.[94] Instead, Paul was attuning Christians to the culture in Corinth that automatically devalued a man whose hair had what the city considered a disreputable, womanly look.[95]

---

[94] Numbers 6:5

[95] Brownson addresses the lowly status of women in the Roman world, "Paul's readers would likely have recalled the assumption, widely attested throughout the ancient world that it was not only unnatural but also inherently shameful and degrading for a man to be reduced to the status

Paul uses phusin to refer to expected individual and societal norms, "natural characteristics, or disposition."[96] Martti Nissinen reflects that it is neither how the male and female sex organs fit nor the majority attraction of male and female that determines what can be considered natural. He asserts that for Paul, naturalness is what comes naturally in a time-bound individual or society. Brownson agrees, saying, "Nature in the ancient world included one's individual or personal nature."[97] It refers to consistent expectations of a person or event. Further, he elaborates, "References to nature in ancient sexual ethics bring us back to... one's individual nature and nature defined as established social order (including gender roles)."[98] Phusin in ancient Rome did not indicate the will of a creator but what ancient Roman society expected. Paul did not teach that same-sex marriage should be avoided as against God's will.

---

of a female by playing the passive role in sexual intercourse. Such a violation of socially established hierarchies was understood to be shocking and dangerous. Indeed, Paul's reference to the "due penalty" that males received for their error (Rom. 1: 27) underscores the social anxiety and instability that such behavior engendered in the ancient world." Brownson, *Bible, Gender, Sexuality*, 245.

[96] Frederick W. Danker, Walter Bauer, and William F. Arndt, "φύσις," *A Greek-English lexicon of the New Testament and other early Christian literature* 869-870.

[97] The intent to procreate was also a cultural expectation of the times. Brownson, *Bible, Gender, Sexuality*, 245-246.

[98] Brownson, *Bible, Gender, Sexuality*, 243-244.

Paul Believed The Embodiment Of All Humans Requires Eroticism

Flash: humans have a body. They must be treated as embodied. They are spirit with body united. Though the nature of the unity is hard to comprehend, Jesus' posture on the cross reminds us of his physical "embrace embodied in Christ's outstretched arms."[99] As well, "humans participate in the transforming event of resurrection as the embodied persons."[100] Paul preaches that Christians should act embodied, "Glorify God with your body." (1 Cor 6:20). Paul condemns the out-of-balance embodiment shown by those who "exchanged the glory of the immortal God for an image resembling mortal human beings"... and "worshiped and served the creation rather than the creator." To not serve the good Creator leaves nothing to serve but something not good." (Romans 1: 23-25) God's will is the embodiment of his spirit in a human package of hopes and physical needs. When body and soul are within God's purpose, embodiment, God's way is realized.

Neither Richard Hays nor Robert Gagnon understands embodiment. Strangely, Richard Hays rejects only the act of homosexuality, not lust. Hays says, for example, "The church should continue to teach—as it always has—that there are two possible ways for God's human sexual creatures to live well-ordered lives of faithful discipleship: heterosexual marriage and sexual

---

[99] Megan K. DeFranza. *Sex Difference in Christian Theology*, p. 4.
[100] Ibid. 238.

abstinence."[101] What, then, does one do with bodily needs? Robert Gagnon writes that the act of celibacy adequately pleases God irrespective of desire, "Scripture presents only two choices for obtaining sexual intercourse: become involved in a lifelong monogamous heterosexual relationship or remain celibate."[102] The two have not fully understood that our united duality is not accidental. God has united body and soul as one.

Taking Hays' and Gagnon's advice would prohibit the sex act but condone burning desire. According to that thinking, an outward change from radically careless sex to abstinence without a change in heart would be acceptable to God. Yet Paul would disagree with that approach for at least two different reasons. Paul sees unfulfilled sexual passions as a hindrance to living.[103] Paul is not content to leave the word lust as a neutral state, but he strengthens it with the descriptors "shameful," "inflamed," and "depraved" of mind. Thus, the sort of lust Paul brings to the minds of his readers is like a secretly fanned flame behind the back of one's acquaintances. Paul's readers know that extreme desire propels the God-forsakers of Romans 1. Romans 1:29-32 doubles down on the evil of their interior life, while also calling into account their inevitable outward deeds. So the key to Romans 1 is not just what God's resistors do but who they are inwardly. We have not found from the Bible that the inner character of a same-sex married couple is deficient. Finally, a practical

---

[101] Richard B. Hays, *The Moral Vision of the New Testament,* Kindle edition, 402.

[102] Robert Gagnon, *The Bible and Homosexual Practice,* Kindle edition, ch. IV.IV.

[103] Romans 1:24-25

stumbling block remains if lust is accepted as an appropriate feeling. How is the sexually inflamed person supposed to be their best self? Are humans designed to operate under such pressure?

Marriage is God's prescription. No marriage is perfect. But it is important to notice that Paul does not condemn either transgender or cisgender, whose sexual expression comes with an inner desire to lastingly support and love another.

The Bible does not condemn same-sex marriage, but tradition sometimes steps beyond the canon. The *Catholic Catechism* published as recently as 1994 supports human tradition over research while yet calling their base Sacred Scripture. It reads as follows.

> Basing itself on Sacred Scripture, which presents homosexual acts as acts of grave depravity, tradition has always declared that homosexual acts are intrinsically disordered. They are contrary to natural law. They close the sexual act to the gift of life. They do not proceed from a genuine affective and sexual complementarity. Under no circumstances can they be approved.[104]

The paragraph is heavy with inaccuracy. The *Catechism* misunderstands the word natural. Neither have its writers dug deeply into the meaning of "lyings of a woman." As well, we have shown that sexual activity that does not procreate is not out of God's will. What is more, sexual relations do not violate God's

---

[104] Catechism of the Catholic Church 2357, http://www.vatican.va/archive/ccc_css/archive/catechism/p3s2c2a6.htm.

will if they do not include complementary genders. We have set the roots of these things out for all to peruse.

Paul recognizes human embodiment as a complex reality in which sexuality furnishes an undeniable drive. Therefore he advises, "It is better to marry than to burn with passion." (1 Cor 7:9). His pronouncement recognizes the essential value of sexual activity for human well-being. How could we deny LGBTQ people the well-being that, according to Paul, is God's intention?

Are LGBTQ people evil? People must be observers of people. With all of decent humanity, LGBTQ people who want to be part of Jesus and his churches will condemn the thoughts and deeds that Paul condemns. Are the LGBTQ we know living in the sewer of verses 29-32? Evangelicals must follow logic. The following logical test applies to the same-sex marriage issue. If expressing homosexuality through a marriage inevitably leads to evil deeds, but those evil deeds are not present in an LGBTQ couple or individual; it follows that expressing homosexuality does not inevitably lead to the evil deeds on Paul's list. To say it another way, if it is logical that if some "B" requires "A," but "A" does not exist, then "B" does not exist either. "B" was contingent on "A," but "A" is not there. Homosexual studies have failed to show that "A," evil acts are uniquely characteristic of LGBTQ individuals; therefore, "B," homosexuals cannot be said to produce evil uniquely. As a result, Paul must not be condemning homosexual acts within a same-sex marriage. Paul is condemning something else. What is Paul condemning in Romans 1? Verses 1:18-25 provide the context we need. Paul frames the perpetrator not as one attracted to the same sex but as one turning their back on God. Logically, the LGBTQ person or a couple of faith is free from this condemnation.

Paul wrote Romans 1-2 to illustrate to Christian Jews that they were just as guilty before God as the Gentiles, even though Gentiles had no divinely given law. The Jews violated the Law God gave to them.[105] Paul writes a rhetorical goad intended to temporarily elevate the indignity of Jewish-Christian hearers against Gentile practices and then shock the self-righteous among them into owning their sin by equating Jewish behavioral offenses with that of those who lived without Law. Romans 1 looks at the Roman elite and does not find the Jews much different. To imagine Paul railing against transsexuals is to go beyond Paul's intent.

In Romans 1, Paul teaches that putting God out of mind leads to perverse extremes. In a genuinely Christian marriage, out-of-control lust will not drive sexuality. Such shameless selfishness is not natural; that is to say, it is not the expected behavior in mutual treasuring.[106] Furthermore, who can say that a depraved mind, as described in Romans 1:29, has been observed to typify same-sex, Jesus-seeking couples?

---

[105] Romans 2:11–27
[106] Romans 1:28

Mistranslations Of Paul In 1 Corinthians 6:9 And 1 Timothy 1:10 Stigmatize LGBTQ

The New International Version's "Men who have sex with men" is a failed translation of *arsenokoitai* and *malakos* in 1 Corinthians 6:9-10. Likewise, "those practicing homosexuality" mistranslates arsenokoitai in 1 Timothy 1:10. Recent translations uniformly attend too little to the analysis of these words. In both cases interpreting the meaning demands four foci: 1) the construction of the Greek word, 2) the word's ancient usage, 3) the placement of the words within lists, and 4) the words in cultural context.

The construction of arsenokoitai combines two Greek words: the word for male and the word for bed. The bed acts as a metaphor for a sexual act. The blended word alone does not indicate whether a male does the bedding or a male is the object of the bedding. In fact, it would be possible for the two words together to signify something that is not a sexual experience. For example, a government official might be said to be in bed with a corporate donor without sexual involvement. To give another example, Daniel Helminiak notes that a man who seems to attract women could be called a "lady killer," two common words that, when together, do not suggest murder.[107] As another, Dale Martin uses the word, understanding, to explain the complexity of word combinations. Martin proposes that neither under nor stand

---

[107] Lings, K. Renato. Love Lost in Translation: Homosexuality and the Bible (p. 503). Trafford Publishing. Kindle Edition.

Steven E. Eike

leads convincingly to the meaning of understand. Similarly, the word combination arsenokoitai does not explain itself.

How was arsenokoitai used in ancient times? Arsenokoitai does not occur in existing records before Paul uses it. If Paul invented the word, it seems reasonable to assume he may have combined two separate words found in both Leviticus 18:22 and 20:13 in the Septuagint, *arsenos* (male) and *koitei* (bed). In Leviticus, both verses state the case against incest, not homosexual eroticism. Jacob also uses the phrase (Gen 45:4) to condemn the incest of his son Reuben with the patriarch's concubine Bilhah (Gen 35:22) to indicate a case of heterosexual incest. The heterosexual event involving Ruben prohibits the two words from requiring a homosexual affair. Consequently, if Paul combined arsenos and koitei from his knowledge of the Greek Old Testament, he assuredly did not have a committed homosexual pairing in mind. After all, the context in 1 Corinthians is incest. (1 Cor 5:1)

In writings other than the Pauline Epistles, the balance of evidence heavily tilts toward arsenokoitai as a term describing exploitation that may or may not be sexual. Frequently it is used to describe dominating another in an unequal power balance. Dale Martin explores the works of authors who employed arsenokoitai early in the first millennium to evaluate meaning. Martin's view is "It is certainly possible, I think probable, that arsenokoités [a cognate of arsenokoitai] referred to a particular role of exploiting others through sex, perhaps but not necessarily by homosexual sex."[108]

---

[108] Dale B. Martin, "Arsenokoites and Malakos: Meanings and Consequences," In *Biblical Ethics and Homosexuality: Listening to Scripture*, ed. Robert L. Brawley, 117-36. Louisville, Kentucky: Westminster John Knox, 1996.

Arsenokoitai turns up, as well, in the non-Pauline *Pseudo-Sibylline Oracles*. Sibyl's composition dates have not been firmly established but may come as early as the time of Paul. [109] From Book II, line 73, Milton S. Terry translated the word to indicate unrighteous, siting: "Cast [not] out the poor unrighteously" in keeping with the context of advantage possibly misused.[110] His paraphrase hopes for fair dealings with others despite having an advantage over them. Hence Milton sees no sexual context in line 73.

> 70 Imperishable honor always first,
> And next thy parents. Render all things due,
> And into unjust judgment come thou not.
> [73] Do not cast out the poor unrighteously,
> Nor judge by outward show; if wickedly
> 75 Thou judgest, God hereafter will judge thee.
> Avoid false testimony; tell the truth.

---

[109] The tradition of the Sibyl as a prophetess dates from as far back as at least 400 BC. Jewish tradition has her as a daughter-in-law of Noah though many nations had prophets in the Sibylline style. The versions on hand likely include some prophecies from the original Sibyls but have had much material added, hence the description as pseudo-Sibylline. The Sibylline Oracles were not accepted into the Christian canon although they were much appreciated. J. J. Collins, "Sibylline Oracles – A New Translation and Introduction by J. J. Collins." In *The Old Testament Pseudepigrapha –Apocalyptic Literature and Testaments, vol. 1,* edited by James H. Charlesworth, (Peabody, MA: Yale University Press, 1983), 317-334.

[110] Milton S. Terry, "The Sibylline Oracles - Sacred-Texts.com," sacred-texts.com (N.Y., NY: Eaton and Mains, 1899, December 2001), https://sacred-texts.com/cla/sib/sib.pdf, 17.

Maintain thy virgin purity, and guard
Love among all. Deal measures that are just;
For beautiful is measure full to all.
80 Strike not the scales one side,
but draw them equally.[111]

The section where we find the cognate, arsenokoitein, in-
structs against abusing the disadvantaged, without a specifically
sexual emphasis.

An imbalance of power rather than homosexuality is again
clear from J. J. Collins' more literal translation. He labels lines 56
through 78 "On Justice" (although he paradoxically translates arsenokoitein as homosexuality in defiance to his section heading).

[70] Never accept in your hand a gift which derives
from unjust deeds. Do not steal seeds. Whoever
takes for himself is accursed to generations of
generations, to the scattering of life. [73] Do not
practice homosexuality [Do not arsenokoitein.
That is: do not take unfair advantage.], do not
betray information, do not murder. Give one who
has labored his wage. Do not oppress a poor man.
Take heed of your speech. Keep a secret matter
in your heart. Make provision for orphans and
widows, and those in need. [78] Do not be willing
to act unjustly, and therefore do not give leave to
one who is acting unjustly.[112]

---

[111] Ibid.

[112] For simplicity, I have eliminated markings indicating document sources.
J. J. Collins, "Sibylline Oracles – A New Translation and Introduction by

It does not make sense to translate arsenokoitein as homo-sexuality in line 73. If the prohibition of all homosexuality were to be the correct understanding of line 73, it would make an isolated sexual prohibition within a section that prohibits injustice related to the public sphere. But an isolated reference to sexual activity does not fit the theme of that section. In another passage of the oracles that lists wrongful sexual behavior, arsenokoitein is absent (Book 2: 279-282).[113] Therefore, it is nowhere near clear that the Sibyl had simple same-sex eroticism in mind. The context shows that Sibyl does not equate the word arsenokoitein with genuine same-sex expressions of love. The better suggestion is that the Sibyl condemns abuse of the vulnerable, an abuse that is not necessarily sexual.

In the second century, non-Pauline *Acts of John,* Section 36 uses arsenokoitai in the context of evil deeds that warrant eternal

---

J. J. Collins." In *The Old Testament Pseudepigrapha –Apocalyptic Literature and Testaments, vol. 1,* edited by James H. Charlesworth, (Peabody, MA: Yale University Press, 1983), 347.

[113] Gagnon mentions two other occasions in the Oracles where sexual immorality influences the context, however in neither case is the word arsenokoitein used: 3.185-87, which he dates ca. 165-45 B.C.E., saying "the author may indeed have had in mind homosexual intercourse with boys" and 5.430 which he believes again refers to "unlawful love of boys." He further comments that Philo had disgust for homosexual intercourse for same-sex intercourse primarily. . . [because of] the passive partner's willingness to discard his masculine nature. Gagnon's comment that *Sib. Or.* borrows 2.73 and many surrounding verses from *Pseudo-Phocylides,* (written between 100 BCE and 100 CE) does nothing to clarify the meaning of arsenokoitein. In this author's view, *Pseudo-Phocylides* may reflect turn-of-the-millennium Jewish prejudice. Robert Gagnon, *The Bible and Homosexual Practice,* Kindle edition, ch. IV, p. 341-342.

Steven E. Eike

condemnation. Although sodomites fall into the context, the biblical view of the sin of Sodom is pride, not homosexual sex. M. R. James, an early twentieth-century scholar translates Section 36.

> Thou that rejoicest in gold and delightest thyself with ivory and jewels, when night falleth, canst thou behold what thou lovest?.... Likewise also thou poisoner, sorcerer, robber, defrauder, sodomite, thief, and as many as are of that band, ye shall come at last, as your works do lead you, unto unquenchable fire.[114]

We do not know James' translation rationale for his inclusion of the word sodomite. We notice, however, that every other word in the context relates to general morality and not homosexual offense.[115] The section preceding 36 deals, in passing, with adultery, but like Section 36, the core of the passage is a rebuke of exploitation of advantage. Adultery abused the abandoned woman by removing her sustenance and stigmatizing her life.

We continue to evaluate the word arsenokoitais. Early in the Christian era, Hippolytus of Rome (CE 170-236) uses arsenokoitai in *The Refutation of All Heresies*, a heretical gnostic "Fall" myth.

---

[114] M.R. James, *Acts of John*, 1924, 36.

[115] We have two complications to observe in determining what M.R. James meant to convey by the word sodomite. Did James understand that sodomites sinned in their arrogant desire to humiliate outsiders rather than from homosexual lust? In other words, did he consider arsenokoités as the act of arrogance it was or instead as a wrong sexual orientation in the way contemporary American culture holds? Two, was he looking for a way out of a translator's dilemma by falling back on a common but incomplete rendering?

In this myth, Satan, whom the tale called Naas, went in unto Eve, deceiving her, and debauched her; and (such an act as) this is a violation of law. He, however, likewise went in unto Adam and had unnatural intercourse with him... whence have arisen adultery and sodomy [arsenokoitais].[116]

Martin amends the translation of Peter Kirby to "possessed him a boy [or a slave].[117] It seems clear that a homosexual act can be described as arsenokoitai when it involves using power to unfair advantage, but also that arsenokoitai does not equate with expressing eroticism within monogamous same-sex marriage.

Pederasty was used to humiliate in ancient times. Bardesanes (died c. 222) wrote of the distaste for pederasty, saying, "From the Euphrates River all the way to the ocean in the East, a man who is derided as a murderer or thief will not be the least bit angry; but if he is derided as an arsenokoités, he will defend himself to the point of murder."[118] The accusation of pederasty is behind the defense of Valerius Asiaticus against his political enemy when accused of feminine softness. He used the accusation of pederasty to shame his enemy, Suillius, by accusing the man's sons. "Ask your sons, Suillius; they'll testify that I'm a man."[119] Pederasty humiliated its victims. Bardesanes used arsenokoités

---

[116] Peter Kirby, "Hippolytus of Rome," *Early Christian Writings*, (Aug. 2021). http//earlychristianwritings.com/text/hippolytus10.

[117] Dale B. Martin, "Arsenokoites and Malakos: Meanings and Consequences," In *Biblical Ethics and Homosexuality: Listening to Scripture*, 1996.

[118] Dale B. Martin, "Arsenokoites and Malakos: Meanings and Consequences," In *Biblical Ethics and Homosexuality: Listening to Scripture*, 1996.

[119] Amy Richlin, "Not before Homosexuality," 538.

to point to the depraved cultural practice of pederasty but not to homosexual eroticism within a committed, life partnership.

Evidence points to pederasty, not LGBTQ, as the evil despised in the ancient Middle East and reported in Romans. In *The Apologies of Aristides* (mid-second century C.E.), the author criticizes Zeus' sexual behavior as arsenokoites because Zeus "carried off the handsome shepherd boy Ganymede to be his 'beloved'."[120] The specific crime is the unequal power balance inherent to pederastic abuse. Yet Gagnon wrongly identifies Zeus' pederasty with any same-sex eroticism. In so doing, he labels all same-sex relationships as evil. But the mythical relationship between Zeus and Ganymede clearly and specifically exemplifies pederasty rather than general homosexuality.

Among Gagnon's errors is relying too much on material written several hundred years after Jesus. In the Christian era, interpreters began to de-emphasize or adjust Jesus' words to fit their worldview. Gagnon's examples are from those days, the fourth and fifth centuries.[121] Our investigations have failed to demonstrate the validity of Gagnon's broad condemnation of all same-sex eroticism. Instead, we reach the understanding of Martin, "I suggest that a careful analysis of the actual context of the use of arsenokoités, free from linguistically specious arguments from etymology or the word's separate parts, indicates that arsenokoités had a different meaning in [first century] Greco-Roman culture than homosexual penetration in general."[122] In 1 Timothy 1:9-10, arsenokoitais does not equate to same-sex eroticism. The

---

[120] Robert A. J. Gagnon, *The Bible and Homosexual Practice*, 344.

[121] Ibid. 344-5.

[122] Dale B. Martin, "Arsenokoites and Malakos: Meanings and Consequences," In *Biblical Ethics and Homosexuality: Listening to Scripture*, 1996.

word, arsenokoitai, stands between the two phrases, sexually immoral and slave traders, two phrases involving domination. The bordering words suggest controlling a person's body for self-gratifying purposes, "the law is made not for the righteous but for lawbreakers and rebels... for the sexually immoral, for those practicing homosexuality [arsenokoitai], for slave traders." The position of arsenokoitai in the list influences our understanding of its meaning. Arsenokoitai must agree with its two companion words which indicate a power-based abusive behavior. The context reveals a scene portraying dominance for advantage.

Abusive control is also the meaning of arsenokoites in Corinthians 6 where Paul addresses the incest topic he began in chapter 5. He uses arsenokoitai in 1 Corinthians 6:9-10, where he clearly had in mind Leviticus 18 and 20 of the LXX. Those chapters testify that incest abuses the family. Where the K.J.V. speaks of abomination, incest is that abomination. Homosexual expression in toto is off the table in Paul's words to the Corinthians. Paul's teaching there does not condemn same-sex marriage. His emphasis falls on incest.

Arsenokoites occurs in combination with malakos. Poor word choices in the N.I.V. seems to cast blame on homosexual eroticism at the point where in 1 Corinthians 6:9 they translate the phrase malakoi and arsenokoitai as "men who have sex with men," a translation that arbitrarily unites the two words to make one meaning. Whatever the meaning, it must represent a significant evil to be placed near idolators and adulterers. The basic sense of the word malakos is softness, as in Matthew 11:8, "men in soft raiment." K.J.V. [123] Perhaps apathetic would be a good word choice. Arsenokoitai speaks, as always, of exploiting a power

---

[123] Thayer and Strong

imbalance. The translation apathetic and abusive fits the basic meaning of the two words. In any case, there is no justification for condemning same-sex eroticism as does the NIV.

Further light is cast upon arsenokoitai by its position in sin lists. Important in determining meaning within sin lists is the meaning of neighboring words. Ancient sin lists group similar sins. We seek, therefore, the similar characteristics of the sin list that contains arsenokoitai. The grouping of the sin list of Section 36 in *Acts of John* (See above.) supports our understanding that same-sex eroticism is not the focus of arsenokoitai. The similarity is an abusive advantage. In 36, the poisoner has the advantage of anonymity, the sorcerer's advantage is human gullibility, the robber has hiddenness, the defrauder does secret plotting, and the thief hides with deviousness, but if arsenokoitais were to be mutual same-sex affection, it implies no abuse of power unless that couple's relationship is abusive. In sum, *Acts of John* condemns abuse of power but does not show a direct link between sin and a loving, same-sex, monogamous life relationship.

Theophilus of Antioch (second century) positioned arsenokoites in a list of what he considered like sins: sexual sins first, next came sins of greed, next arsenokoites, and then sins of uncontrolled emotions. He used the word arsenokoites in his *To Autolycus,* to describe corrupting of boys.[124] In the list, arsenokoites stands between greed and lack of emotional control, but its position is distant from any mention of sexual sin. In its "in-between" place, arsenokoites cannot easily be defined by context. Kirby translates it pederasty, an ugly cultural practice of the Roman world,[125] but

---

[124] Peter Kirby, "Theophilus To Autolycus," *Early Christian Writings* (Aug. 2021). http//earlychristianwritings.com/text/theopolis-book1html.
[125] Ibid.

that is likely too specific a meaning for its position in the list. A translation that indicates general abuse is more appropriate.

In sum, the sin lists in 1 Corinthians Chapters five and six support a realm of meaning for malakos and arsenokoites that is not sexual. In the two chapters are three sin lists.[126] All start with the word for sexual immorality, *pornos*. That is natural since Paul deals with incest within the church. The first and second lists exclude any other words that key on sexual sins. In the third and longest list, 1 Corinthians 6:9-10, Paul places malakos and arsenokoitai directly in the middle. In everyday use of these two words, apathetic and abusive, they reflect attitudes that promote any vice. They occupy the center, expressing the core of vice: weakness of character and desire to exploit. They do not specifically call out sexual evil and they incriminate neither same-sex marriage nor homosexual attraction.

Coitus does not always mean coitus in certain cultures. It should be obvious that even in English, coitus does not always mean sexual intercourse. It is, therefore, not true that the combined words, male and bed [or coitus], must refer to a sexual act. English has a clear example of a blatantly sexual word used asexually. It is the "f" word. A person being manipulated may say, "Stop 'f-ing' with me"! A person who is perpetually confused might be called "f-ed" up. How mystifying that would be to a person who does not speak English! In the United States, we speak a language foreign to the koine Greek of the Roman day. We of the present day should be more careful about our interpretation. Our extreme literal understanding of it is all "f"-ed up. Arsenokoites, like the English "f" word, does not always mean coitus.

---

[126] 5:10, 5:11, 6:9-10

JESUS HELPS AND APPRECIATES LGBTQ CHOICES

Jesus was radical for God in his day, and so he is in ours. Amid the first century's sex prejudices and fears, he blessed the different. In Matthew 19, Jesus repeated God's desire for total marital fidelity to the astonished disciples. Marriage was to be considered a serious thing, the originating of a new family. Using the culturally assumed asexuality of eunuchs, he described that only the eunuch was exempt from complete faithfulness in marriage because they were not considered marriageable. He went on, nevertheless, to tell the blessed state of the eunuch. While in a former day, Israel excluded the sexually different from nearness to God in the temple, yet Jesus himself, the fullness of the temple, declared their welcome into God's intimacy.[127] He says, "There are those who choose to live like eunuchs for the sake of the kingdom of heaven." Matt. 19:12 To Jesus, the sexually different eunuch could live for God and come close to God.

---

[127] Matthew 19:12

Eunuchs were well-known in the first century. According to Miners and Conneley, first-century eunuchs "as a class had a reputation for being attracted sexually to men, rather than women." [128] When Jesus refers to eunuchs who were born that way," these eunuchs possessed what today would be called LGBTQ characteristics. Signs of natural eunuchs [eunuchs from the womb] are [were] said to include lateness of pubic hair, urine that does not form an arch, absence of a beard, softness of hair, smoothness of skin, a high voice, and a body that does not steam when bathing in winter.[129] In addition, those who were for whatever reason considered incapable of fathering children were considered eunuchs.[130] Again, today these qualities might call up the label LGBTQ.

Besides eunuchs from birth were man-made eunuchs. These were often chosen by wealthy and ruling families to be charged with the harem, to care for them without using them sexually. This approach to chastity for the harem may have occasionally failed, as suggested in a recent study of castrated men, many of whom were in a sexual relationship with a woman.[131] Nevertheless, lack of sexual interest in women by castrated men was the assumption of Jesus' day and the assumption ruled in conversation. Their assumed asexuality would have influenced

---

[128] Jeff Miner and John Tyler Conneley, *The Children are Free: Reexamining the Biblical Evidence on Same-sex Relationships*, Indianapolis, IN: Jesus Metropolitan Community Church, 2002, Kindle Version 528-529 of 1098.

[129] Ibid. 525-527.

[130] Ibid. 547.

[131] Wibowo, Erik, Samantha T S Wong, Richard J. Wassersug, and Thomas W Johnson. "Sexual Function After Voluntary Castration." Archives of sexual behavior. 50, no. 8 (2021): 3889–3899.

Jesus' dialog about divorce and marriage. No one was likely to think gays had heterosexual marriage interests.

Jesus had a message of full inclusion and acceptance within his kingdom. Jesus declared that a heterosexual might make themselves sexually different for the glory of God, there are those who choose to live like eunuchs for the sake of the kingdom of heaven. (Matt. 19:12, N.I.V.) The King James Version is less paraphrastic, "eunuchs, which [sic] have made themselves eunuchs." In other words, some may have lived as a eunuch, celibate, for the glory of God. Others had themselves castrated. They became unacceptable to their culture but acceptable to glorify God. Jesus acknowledged the value of their sacrifice.

Why did Jesus bring up that "the Creator made them male and female" and the two would become one flesh? Matthew 19:4-5 He was bringing to the minds of the Pharisee accusers that marriage was a unity with vulnerable people. Pharisees often treated their partner as a non-entity who could be cast off without further responsibility. Hence their question, "Is it lawful for a man to divorce his wife for any and every reason?" Matthew 19:3 God's desire for marriage is a new forever family. He then asks if they can physically meet the criteria to accept God's word about marriage. He implies that the gay have a spiritual advantage over them. Matthew 19:11-12 The sayings lift up the gay community and put down the pride of the abusive Pharisees.

Jesus did good fearlessly. In a fearless show of acceptance, Jesus quickly and without question helped a centurion whose dearly loved (*centimos*) child servant (*pais*) was on their deathbed.[132] The centurion says to him, "Lord, don't trouble yourself, for I do not deserve to have you come under my roof. That is

---

132 Luke 7

why I did not even consider myself worthy to come to you. But say the word and my servant will be healed." Jesus healed the young beloved whose situation would have brought the evil of pederasty to the mind of Bible readers of the day. Elite Roman soldiers frequently "mentored" young boys and used them sexually. We have no certain information that it was the case with this centurion. The reader is left only with suspicions. Luke courageously records no rebuke by Jesus. Jesus healed the boy. Gender preference does not prohibit God from helping without embarrassing.

NEW TESTAMENT ETHICS SUPPORT SAME-SEX MARRIAGE

God values same-sex marriage. Just as God provided a suitable partner for Adam so that he would have the basics he needed for success, he wants all his beloved to have the essential support they need.[133] Unless we are willing to say that he gifts all LGBTQ with celibacy, then in fairness, God must ethically allow them a sexual outlet through marriage. If LGBTQ had no sexual interest, we would not be having this discussion, but God has given bodies to all human beings. Consequently, a healthy relationship needs expression in the body. Living holistically involves hugs and kisses, physical displays of affection, and other forms of nurturing and building that make successful humans. Brownson aptly remarks, "Scripture clearly links sexual expression with one-flesh union that establishes lifelong, stable kinship ties."[134]

Each marriage represents a new opportunity for a jubilee. The new couple has the joyful chance to make right the hardness

---

[133] Gen 2:18

[134] Brownson, James V. Bible, Gender, Sexuality (220).

of the past through their commitment to love one another and their neighbor. Brownson makes a solid argument that marriage makes a new kinship unit separate from the family of origin. He calls it a "realignment of kinship ties."[135] He points to the Hebrew lexical meaning of flesh (*basar*) as relatives, and so it follows that the Genesis writer refers to the creation of a new group of relatives, a family, a fresh start to a people and an earth that would need repair.[136]

---

[135] Ibid, Sexuality (33).
[136] Ibid.

SUMMARY: THE NEW TESTAMENT ON SAME-SEX MARRIAGE

- The empire's culture posed sexual threats to first-century Christians.
- First-century Christians inherited a prejudiced worldview of Jews toward Gentiles.
- Word study shows Paul to use *phusin* (natural) to refer to expectation rather than to describe an eternal standard.
- Paul stands against the depraved element of Roman culture in Romans 1, but not against same-sex marriage. He tells the Jewish Christians, who still tend to judgmentalism, that they are not better than Roman Christ-followers.
- In 1 Corinthians 6:9 and 1 Timothy 1:10, Paul refers to incest and pederasty rather than same-sex intimacy.
- The sin lists in 1 Corinthians Chapters 5 and 6 support a realm of meaning for malakos and arsenokoites that is not sexual.
- Word study shows that Paul combines arsenos and koitai to mean abusive dominance of any type.

- Jesus highly regarded the LGBTQ of his time. Jesus encouraged them. He did not rebuke them.
- Luke, as a disciple of Christ, courageously recorded Jesus' care of LGBTQ.
- God's goodness could be impugned if he did not gift the same-sex inclined with celibacy.
- The human body is a part of God's creation that needs ministry.

CONCLUSION

God has hallowed faithful same-sex marriage. Spiritually minded people have heard God's silent voice to move toward justice for LGBTQ. The notice has gone out that frozen scholarship must look closer at God's word. Universities must respond. The best research must seek to penetrate the ancient cultures to factor in the worldviews that influenced the old influencers Bible study relies on. Those gifted with words and understanding must teach.

Both ancient Judaism and contemporary Christianity have failed us. Both have yet to do the required job to flesh out the truth about LGBTQ and live by it. Ro 2:1 Church events show many evangelicals to abusively dominate through their calcified tradition. This book shows they have not reviewed their core beliefs. There is no time for such lack of due-diligence. Shepherds of courage and vision must stand to lead today's clearly struggling humanity.

BIBLIOGRAPHY

Achtemeier, Mark. *The Bible's Yes to Same-Sex Marriage: Change of Heart.* Louisville, KY: Westminster John Knox Press, 2015.

Aristotle. *Generation of Animals.* Vol. 366. Translated by A. L. Peck. Cambridge, MA: Harvard University Press, 2014.

Balla, Peter. "2 Corinthians." In *Commentary on the New Testament Use of the Old Testament*, edited by G. K. Beale and D. A. Carson, 752–783. Grand Rapids, MI: Baker Academic, 2007.

Boswell, John. *Boswell, John and History E-Book Project. Christianity, Social Tolerance, and Homosexuality: Gay People in Western Europe from the Beginning of the Christian Era to the Fourteenth Century.* Paperback ed. Chicago: University of Chicago Press, 1981.

Brownson, James V. *Bible, Gender, Sexuality: Reframing the Church's Debate on Same-Sex Relationships.* Grand Rapids, MI: William B. Eerdmans Publishing Company, 2013.

Budin, Stephanie Lynn and Jean MacIntosh Turfa. *Women in Antiquity: Real Women Across the Ancient World*. London; New York: Routledge, 2016.

Collins, J. J., "Sibylline Oracles – A New Translation and Introduction by J. J. Collins." In *The Old Testament Pseudepigrapha – Volume 1 Apocalyptic Literature and Testaments*, edited by James H. Charlesworth, 317-472. Peabody, MA: Yale University Press, 1983.

Danker, Frederick W., Walter Bauer, and William F. Arndt. 1979. *A Greek-English lexicon of the New Testament and other early Christian literature*.

DeFranza, Megan K. *Sex Difference in Christian Theology: Male, Female, and Inter-sex in the Image of God*. Grand Rapids, MI: Wm. B. Eerdmans, 2015. Kindle edition.

Elwell, Walter A. and Robert W. Yarbrough, *Encountering the New Testament: A Historical and Theological Survey*, 3rd ed. in Encountering Biblical Studies. Grand Rapids, MI: Baker Publishing Group, 2013. Kindle edition.

Flory, Marleen Boudreau. "Caligula's 'Inverecundia': A Note on Dio Cassius 59.12.1." *Hermes* 114, no. 3 (1986): 365-71. Accessed January 2, 2021. http://www.jstor.org/stable/4476511.

Foucault, Michel, and Robert. Hurley. *The History of Sexuality* First Vintage books edition. New York, NY: Vintage Books, 1988.

Gagnon, Robert A. *The Bible and Homosexual Practice: Texts and Hermeneutics*. Nashville, TN: Abingdon Press, Kindle edition.

Grenz, Stanley J. *Welcoming but Not Affirming: an Evangelical Response to Homosexuality.* Louisville, KY: Westminster John Knox Press, 1998.

Gutierrez, Bejarano Juan Marcos. *The Transformation of Israelite Religion to Rabbinic Judaism.* Grand Prairie, TX: Yaron Publishing. Kindle Edition

Hartley, John E. *Leviticus,* vol. 4 of the Word Biblical Commentary. Grand Rapids, MI: Zondervan Academic, 1992. Kindle edition.

Hays, Richard B. *The Moral Vision of the New Testament: a Contemporary Introduction to New Testament Ethics.* NY, NY: HarperCollins Publishers, 2013. Kindle edition.

Hill, Andrew E.; Walton, John H. A Survey of the Old Testament (p. 71). Zondervan Academic. Kindle Edition.

James, M. R. 1924. *Acts of John.* Oxford: Clarendon Press. Accessed August 5, 2021. http://www.earlychristianwritings.com/actsjohn.html.

Jobes, Karen H., Silva, Moisés. *Invitation to the Septuagint.* Grand Rapids, MI: Baker Publishing Group, 2015. Kindle edition.

Kirby, Peter. "Hippolytus of Rome," *Early Christian Writings.* Book 10. (Aug. 2021). http//earlychristianwritings.com/text/hippolytus10. Accessed August 2021.

Kirby, Peter. "Theophilus of Antioch – to Autolychus.*Early Christian Writings.* (Aug. 2021). http//earlychristianwritings.com/text/theopolis-book1html. Accessed August 2021.

Kuefler, Matthew. *Masculinity, Gender Ambiguity, and Christian Ideology in Late Antiquity* in the Chicago Series on Sexuality, History and Society. Edited by John C. Fout. Chicago, IL: University of Chicago Press, 2001.

Lings, K Renato. 2009. "The 'Lyings' of a Woman: Male-Male Incest in Leviticus 18.22?" In Theology & Sexuality 15.2 (2009): 231–250. doi:10.1558/tse.v15i2.231.

Martin, Dale B. "Arsenokoites and Malakos: Meanings and Consequences." In *Biblical Ethics and Homosexuality: Listening to Scripture*, ed. Robert L. Brawley, 117-36. Louisville, Kentucky: Westminster John Knox, 1996.

Masterson, Mark. Sex in Antiquity Exploring Gender and Sexuality in the Ancient World. London ; New York: Routledge, 2018. (Edited By Mark Masterson, Nancy Sorkin Rabinowitz, James Robson.)

Miner, Jeff and Conneley, John Tyler. *The Children are Free: Reexamining the Biblical Evidence on Same-sex Relationships*, Indianapolis, IN: Jesus Metropolitan Community Church, 2002

Monge, Janet and Page Selinsky, "Patterns of violence against women in the Iron Age town of Hasanlu, Solduz Valley, Iran Women in Antiquity" in *Women in Antiquity: Real Women across the Ancient World*, ed. Stephanie Lynn Budin and Jean Macintosh Turfa. London: Routledge, 2016. 138–155.

McGinn, Thomas A. *Prostitution, Sexuality, and the Law in Ancient Rome.* 2nd Ed. New York, NY: Oxford University Press, 2003.

Nissinen, Martti. 1998. *Homoeroticism in the biblical world: a historical perspective*. Minneapolis, Minn: Fortress Press.

Niswonger, Richard L. *New Testament History*. Grand Rapids, MI: Zondervan, 1992.

Richlin, Amy. "Not before Homosexuality: The Materiality of the Cinaedus and the Roman Law against Love between Men." *Journal of the History of Sexuality* 3, no. 4 (1993): 523-73. Accessed October 24, 2020. http://www.jstor.org/stable/3704392.

Ringrose, Kathryn M. *The Perfect Servant: Eunuchs and the Social Construction of Gender in Byzantium*. Chicago, IL: University of Chicago Press, 2004.

Sim, David C., and James S. McLaren. Attitudes to Gentiles in Ancient Judaism and Early Christianity London: Bloomsbury T & T Clark, 2014.

Smith, Nicholas D. "Plato and Aristotle on the Nature of Women." *Journal of the History of Philosophy* 21, no. 4 (1983): 467-478.

Sprinkle, Preston M., William R. G. Loader, Megan K. DeFranza, Wesley Hill, Stephen R. Holmes, Stanley H. Gundry, and Megan K DeFranza. "Journeying from the Bible to Christian Ethics in Search of Common Ground." Essay. In *Two Views on Homosexuality, the Bible, and the Church*, 69–123. Grand Rapids, MI: Zondervan, 2016. Kindle edition.

Terry, Milton S. "The Sibylline Oracles - Sacred-Texts.com." sacred-texts.com. N.Y., NY: Eaton and Mains, 1899, December 2001. https://sacred-texts.com/cla/sib/sib.pdf.

Van Seters, John. "Ezra." In *Encyclopedia of Religion*, 2nd ed., edited by Lindsay Jones, 2946-2947. Vol. 5. Detroit, MI: Macmillan Reference U.S.A., 2005. *Gale eBooks* (accessed August 23, 2020). https://link-gale-com.ezproxy.liberty.edu/apps/doc/CX3424500990/GVRL?u=vic_liberty&sid=GVRL&xid=db020e9a.

Vines, Matthew. *God and the Gay Christian: The Biblical Case in Support of Same-Sex Relationships*. First Ed. New York: Convergent Books, 2014.

Walton, John H. *Genesis*. The N.I.V. Application Commentary. Grand Rapids, MI: Zondervan, 2014. Kindle edition.

Wenham, Gordon J. *The Book of Leviticus*. New International Commentary on the Old Testament. Grand Rapids, MI: William B. Eerdmans, 1979.

Wenham, Gordon J. *Rethinking Genesis 1-11: Gateway to the Bible: the Didsbury Lectures 2013*. Eugene, OR: Cascade Books. 2015.

Wenham, Gordon J. *Genesis 1-15 Vol. 1*. Word Biblical Commentary. Grand Rapids, MI: Zondervan, 2017. Kindle edition.

Yamauchi, Edwin M. "Ezra–Nehemiah" in *The Expositor's Bible Commentary*, Ed. Frank E. Gaebelein, 565–771. Grand Rapids, MI: Zondervan, 1977.

Printed in the United States
by Baker & Taylor Publisher Services